Turning the Ship

Exploring the Age-Integrated Church

Why the church needs to demolish age barriers and join together as the family of God

Dustin Guidry

Copyright © 2009 by Dustin Guidry

Turning the Ship
Exploring the Age-Integrated Church
by Dustin Guidry

Printed in the United States of America

ISBN 978-1-60791-262-0

All rights reserved solely by the author. The author guarantees all contents are original and do not infringe upon the legal rights of any other person or work. No part of this book may be reproduced in any form without the permission of the author. The views expressed in this book are not necessarily those of the publisher.

Unless otherwise indicated, Bible quotations are taken from The English Standard Version, Copyright © 2001 by Crossway Bibles, a division of Good News Publishers, and The King James Version of the Bible.

Cover design by churchlogogallery.com.

www.xulonpress.com

To my beautiful wife and children:

*Because you are too precious a cargo,
this journey had to happen.*

To my church family at Ridgewood:

*Because of your love for truth no matter the cost,
this journey has happened.*

Contents

Foreword by Dr. Voddie Baucham .... *ix*
Introduction .... *xiii*

Part 1: The Desperate Need to Turn the Ship 17

1. Houston, We Have a Problem: Realizing the
   Seriousness of the Crisis We Face 19
2. Run, Run as Fast as You Can! Rejecting the
   Secularization of the Church 31
3. Humpty Dumpty Has Been Made Whole! Relying
   on the Sufficiency of Scripture 47
4. The Lights Are Back On! Recapturing Hearts,
   Minds, and Souls 63

Part 2: The Directions for the Journey 73

5. When Men Knew No Better: The Means of
   Church Growth 75
6. E. F. . . . E. F. . . . E. F. Hutton: The Message
   of Church Growth 93
7. My Dad Is Bigger Than Your Dad: The Method
   of Church Growth 105

Part 3: Discoveries from the New Land 117

8. The Big *BUT* Syndrome: The Obstacle That
   Stands in the Way 119
9. The Cookie-Cutter Family: Breaking the Cycle
   of Dysfunction 123
10. Million Dollar Question: The Answer Is No 133
11. What Does the Age-Integrated Church Look
    Like? Masks Have Been Removed and
    Individualism Has Died 141
12. You Can't Buy It in a Box: Where to Go
    from Here 151
13. God Help Me. Amen: Closing Remarks 157

Notes *159*

Foreword

The avalanche of research over the last several years concerning the unbiblical worldviews and mass exodus of church teens has brought great sobriety, fear, and repentance for some, while others have looked at reports from the Barna Group, the National Study of Youth and Religion, the Nehemiah Institute, and the Southern Baptist Council on the Family and merely shrugged their shoulders as though *Turning the Ship* is not an option. Opinions are myriad as to the cause of the disappointing slide. Some blame shallow youth ministries, others point the finger at aggressive college professors, while still others blame the researchers. However, there is universal agreement that something must be done.

The age-segregated youth group is an immovable object; a "sacred cow" if you will, that is destined to remain intact for the foreseeable future. There are myriad voices sounding the alarm for youth ministry reform. Those voices repeat mantras like, "We mustn't overreact," and "We can't throw the baby out with the bathwater." However, one refrain that is noticeably absent is that of, "We must continue to trust the biblical model." Perhaps that is because there is no biblical model for youth ministry.

For nearly 2,000 years the church knew nothing of age segregated ministry. However, to hear youth ministry advocates speak, one would believe that Jesus himself was part of a youth group and age-graded Sunday school. Gone are the voices like George Whitefield, who said:

> [P]ersons are generally very liberal of their invectives against the clergy, and think they justly blame the conduct of that minister who does not take heed to and watch over the flock, of which the Holy Ghost has made him overseer: but may not every governor of a family, be in a lower degree liable to the same censure, who takes no thought for those souls that are committed to his charge? For every house is as it were a little parish, every governor a priest, every family a flock; and if any of them perish through the governor's neglect, their blood will God require at their hands.[1]

Today, such words are foreign to our ears. Gone are the days when Christians understood that the home—and not the Christian church or school—is principally and primarily responsible for the education, evangelism, and discipleship of children and that our ecclesiology should reflect that reality.

In his classic work, *The Reformed Pastor*, Richard Baxter (who, like every other minister of his day, had nothing like our modern age-graded ministries in his church) captured the essence of pastoral responsibility in light of the proper function and role of the Christian home. He wrote:

> What are we like[ly] to do ourselves to the reforming of a congregation, if all the work be cast on [pastors] alone; and masters of families neglect that necessary duty of their own, by which they are bound to help us? If any good be begun by the ministry in any soul, a careless, prayerless, worldly family is [apt] to stifle it, or very much hinder it; whereas, if you could

but get the rulers of families to do their duty, to take up the work where you left it, and help it on, what abundance of good might be done! I beseech you, therefore, if you desire the reformation and welfare of your people, do all you can to *promote family religion.*[2] (emphasis added)

This is not to say that churches and pastors have no role to play. As George Barna notes, the church and the home must play a "symbiotic role" in the development of the next generation. And the home must lead.

That is where Dustin Guidry's work comes in. Dustin has done what many thought was impossible. He has taken a neo-traditional[3] church and moved it toward family integration. In *Turning the Ship,* he offers an honest, hard-hitting, no-holds-barred look at the origins, the path, obstacles, and the tremendous rewards of his church's journey. This is not a panacea. Nor is it a program-oriented marketing scheme designed to get every church on the same path in forty days. This is one man's story of triumph, tragedy, heartache, and joy as he pursued biblical ecclesiology with tenacity that at times resembled Jacob wrestling with the angel.

Turning the Ship is not for the faint of heart. Calling fathers to lead and removing the safety net is no easy task. Nevertheless, as you will read, Dustin Guidry is not a man who looks for the easy way out. His desire through it all was to do what the Bible teaches in regard to the structure and ministry of the local church. The journey is not over. As the reformers aptly noted, we are "always reforming," and this story is no exception. However, the hardest part is done; the ship has been turned. And Dustin Guidry has lived to tell about it.

Dr. Voddie Baucham

Introduction

Discovering New Oceans

I'll never forget the night. Although it was the same as every other night in Southeast Texas with its thick humidity and swarming mosquitoes, this night was different. I was standing outside on the church parking lot talking with a good friend who asked the question, "How are we going to get there?" His question pertained to Ridgewood Church moving toward what has been termed by some *the family-integrated church*. (I will mainly use the terms *age-integrated church* and *multigenerational community* to describe this movement.)

Before we'd ever heard of the age-integrated church movement, we were already moving toward integrating all ages during our church practices. So this question came at a time when we were trying to understand as a body the totality of what God was doing in our midst. Everyone could sense His guiding hand, but we just didn't quite know how to get there or even what the destination would look like. Some members wanted to rock the boat and change course immediately, others wanted to see it happen a little slower, and a few didn't want to go down this path at all. One thing that couldn't be denied was that God wanted something to happen.

When my friend, who falls in the let's-rock-the-boat category, asked me that night, "How are we going to get there?" I answered his question with a question. "If you had a ship full of passengers and you knew that for the people's sake the ship needed to be going in the opposite direction, how would you change course to ensure that most of the passengers would still be riding together in the ship on this new course?"

I told him that if you turned the ship all at once to go the opposite direction, the ship would capsize and there would be a lot of people lost at sea. If on the other hand the risk of any casualties made us too scared to even attempt to turn the ship around, then it would be just a matter of time before the passengers would die off one by one with those remaining forgetting even why they were on the boat in the first place.

The only alternative for us to turn an existing age-segregated church into one that was age integrated was to turn it slowly. Turning the ship slowly would allow for three things. First, due to the fact that the ship was indeed turning, we would ultimately arrive safely at our desired destination. The ship would still be intact. Second, people would not be thrown overboard because of the ship's gradual turning. Instead, if they were to fall and lose their balance on the deck, others would be able to reach out their hands and pick them back up. Third, for those who refused to go with us in the opposite direction from all of the other ships around us, they would have plenty of time to lower themselves down in the lifeboats and wait for any one of those ships to take them in.

Needless to say, the Lord's turning the ship at Ridgewood Church did not take place overnight. Through several years of challenges, trials, and uncontrollable variables, Ridgewood has made the 180-degree turn and is now traveling against the current of both the culture at large and the culture in the church. The ship is intact. The majority are still here. New passengers have boarded the ship. Glory goes to God alone.

This book describes not only the details of Ridgewood's journey but also gives insight into why we, or anyone else for that matter, would risk making the turn at all. Believe me. It would have been a lot easier to drift along with the big mainstream ships, but it would be just that: drifting. Now we are moving full steam ahead with a renewed passion and vigor for a cause that is just, is right, and is God honoring. It is a journey that has been so powerful and transforming that we will continue onward never looking back.

Turning the Ship is a product of the journey. It is written in three parts. Part 1 establishes the desperate need for Christians to turn the ship. Part 2 looks to God and His Word for the directions for this exciting journey. Part 3 has some final thoughts about the discoveries of the new land that we have found during this transition.

No matter if you are a part of an age-integrated church, interested or curious about this movement, have never heard of it, or are dead set against it, my prayer is that you will understand that this movement is not some passing fad or some cool new model. This movement is about seeking integrity and purity in churches across this world. It is about seeing His kingdom come here on earth as it is in heaven. It is about continually being reformed by the eternal truths of God's Word.

The age-integrated church is a movement that is fundamentally different from what we typically have come to know about church in our Western world. This has made writing difficult because often the words that are used to describe church, church practices, or church culture are the same on the surface but have drastic differences in their respective definitions. I hope you can make the distinctions between the words I am using from their context.

Turning the Ship

So, with this said, put on your life jacket and hold on tight. It is time to take this journey together. May you be challenged by an anonymous quote that says:

*You cannot discover new oceans,
unless you have courage to lose sight of the shore.*

Part 1

The Desperate Need to Turn the Ship

Chapter 1

Houston, We Have a Problem
Realizing the Seriousness of the Crisis We Face

*I appeal to you therefore, brothers, by the mercies of God,
to present your bodies as a living sacrifice,
holy and acceptable to God, which is your spiritual
worship. (Romans 12:1)*

Living east of Houston my whole life has been a wonderful experience. All of the advantages of the city life were just a ninety-minute drive away. The advantages of shopping at a galleria, visiting a major zoo, touring many museums and historical sites, dining at restaurants galore, and having the most advanced medical hospitals in the world all paled in light of one singular advantage: the fact that we lived in the television viewing region of a city that had a major sports team in every major sports league. I grew up watching the Astros, the Rockets, and the Luv Ya Blue Oilers. As a young boy who dreamed of playing for one if not all of these franchises, I was oblivious to the many dismal seasons that the Houston teams seemed to have year after year. I could never understand why I would hear adults say things after a disappointing loss like, "I'm never watching these chokers again!"

It wasn't until I was older that I actually understood the significance and meaning of one particular saying that was tirelessly repeated by all of the journalists, sports' commentators, and/or my adult family members concerning the poor play of my favorite childhood Houstonian teams. It was the infamous phrase, "Houston, we have a problem!"

As one who was born after the race to the moon was already won, I always wondered why people said, "Houston, we have a problem!" when the Houston teams ran up against an insurmountable wall. Of course I would one day learn of the heroic story of the Apollo 13 crew where astronaut Jim Lovell radioed those echoing words to the NASA command center in Houston after one of the oxygen tanks in the service module exploded. The explosion happened on the way to the moon and thankfully the crew was able to return to earth safely after enduring unplanned hardships due to the explosion.

While I was in college in 1995, Hollywood brought this unforgettable space mission to the big screen with the motion picture *Apollo 13*. The movie captured the real-life drama that unfolded on April 14, 1970, when the explosion occurred. The anticipation and anxiety of the astronauts, their families, NASA personnel, and the citizens of the entire country were vividly portrayed for all to see firsthand. Tom Hanks said Lovell's words well in the movie: "Houston, we have a problem."

In that nail-biting scene in the movie, we saw the innards of the smoke-filled room of NASA's Mission Control in Houston. During that memorable scene, the Apollo 13 flight director Gene Kranz immediately took over the Mission Control room demanding information, answers, and solutions to the apparent crisis. Kranz calmly asked the poignant question, "Is this an instrumentation problem or are we looking at real power loss here?" knowing that if power was lost, the spacecraft could be lost in space forever.

It is that one line that haunts me today as a Christian father and pastor in the twenty-first century. Sadly it is the one question that must be asked or addressed in light of the problems facing the future of Christianity in our day.

Very few people would argue that the church in America is facing a crisis. The Apollo 13 declaration of "Houston, we have a problem" continues to be echoed again and again and again to all who claim to be followers of Jesus Christ. There seem to be few leaders in Christendom who have the passion and intestinal fortitude to recognize that the problem indeed is a power loss: a Holy Spirit power loss to be exact. This power loss is in the lives of millions of self-ascribed born-again Christians thus directly resulting in a power loss in the biblical family unit and the church. Unless the power system is restored in the church, I am afraid that the faith that has once and for all been delivered to the saints will do nothing more than drift into outer space away from the hopeless inhabitants of the earth.

You may already be saying, "Yeah, yeah. I have heard this drumbeat for the last two decades loud and clear, and I know that there is a problem, *but* . . .!" The infamous big *BUT* syndrome plagues the church in America. (I will address the syndrome in more detail later on in the book). Allow me to state one more time for you that "Christian, we have a problem!" and it is a problem of power loss.

The Power-Loss Problem Diagnosed

The apostle Paul in Romans 12:1 makes an appeal to the Roman brethren that they are to present their "bodies as a living sacrifice, holy and acceptable to God" which he declared was their "spiritual worship" or reasonable service. That same appeal or call is required of believers today some two thousand years later. The problem we now face is that the church at large is not living a life filled with supernatural power that we can honestly say is acceptable to an infinite, holy God. As anyone can see just by examining our day with an honest eye, there is little or no difference in the way people think and live inside the walls of the church compared to those who never attend church. Pollster George Barna reveals that only 9 percent of born-again Christians live and operate from a biblical worldview.[1] That one statistic should be enough, but just in case you have turned a blind eye to the reality surrounding you, I'll list some more statistics to shed light on the crisis.

I believe one of the most telling signs of power loss in Christendom is the lack of ability to pass down the faith to subsequent generations. In his book *The Bridger Generation*, Thom Rainer tracks the number of evangelical Christians in each of the identified generations. The following graph is based on his findings. As you will notice, there has been a drastic decline in the percentage of evangelicals over the last four generations. Christianity statistically is dying off.

Decreasing Numbers of Evangelicals[2]

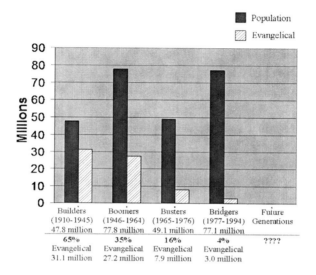

What in the world happened? Why the sudden decrease of Christianity among the young people in our nation? During a time in history when people have unadulterated access to the Bible, to churches on every corner, to Christian books, to Christian media, and to the internet, shouldn't we see an increase in Christianity? Haven't we done all we could do to seek and attract the lost to our churches and even sports arenas by using the most technological advances humankind has ever seen? Surely the increase of our understanding about the human psyche should help us see more people motivated and manipulated to come to Jesus. With all the camps, conferences, and curriculums that are being consumed in our churches and youth ministries, why are we losing 70–88 percent[3] of our young people by their sophomore year in college? This doesn't make any sense!

To add injury to insult, when you take the youngest believers on the spectrum (those who make up the Bridger generation), research shows that their Christianity can hardly be described as biblical or orthodox Christianity. Today's research shows that "accepting Christ" and making a profession of faith today makes little or no difference in a young person's attitudes and behaviors. Josh McDowell reveals the shallow faith of our young people in his book *The Last Christian Generation*. McDowell found the following:

> 63 percent don't believe Jesus is the Son of the one true God.
> 58 percent believe all faiths teach equally valid truths.
> 51 percent don't believe Jesus rose from the dead.
> 65 percent don't believe Satan is a real entity.
> 68 percent don't believe the Holy Spirit is a real entity.[4]

He also stated that there is a 4 percent statistical difference between the behavior and lifestyles of evangelical kids who go to church and those kids who do not attend church. This research indicated the following:

> 74 percent of our churched kids cheat on school tests.
> 83 percent lie to their teachers.
> 93 percent lie to their parents.
> 63 percent become physically violent when angered.[5]

In light of these findings, McDowell rightly makes the following assessment of our young people:

> Much of what they believe about Christianity, truth, reality, and the church comes from a distorted view they have gleaned from around them. It's not that they haven't embraced a version of Christianity; it's simply that the version they believe in is not built on the true foundation of what biblical Christianity is all about.[6]

Will you allow me to say again, "Christian, we have a problem!"?

Have Mercy on Us

The grim results of this research seem to cause a myriad of reactions across Christian circles. Some look at any statistic with skepticism. Others look at these statistics as something that is happening in the Northwest, on the East Coast, or on the West Coast, but not something that is occurring in the Bible Belt or even in their own local church. Others' hearts are so distraught and overwhelmed with the gloomy review these statistics reveal that they are unable to think about the implications, causing them to turn a blind eye toward the problem all together. Still some fight against anyone who tries to use these statistics to challenge the church culture at large in fear of losing power, control, money, or their jobs.

There do, however, appear to be some Joshuas and Calebs in the crowd who understand the daunting task before them and are actually willing to take on the giants that threaten the future of the survival of Christianity in the next generations. Joshua and Caleb were two of the twelve spies that Moses sent out to scope out God's Promised Land for His people in Numbers 13. Because of the giants the Israelites would have to face in the Promised Land, ten of the twelve spies said the task of taking the land was too great. Joshua and Caleb were the only two who wanted to follow the Lord's directive and take possession of the land. Sadly, Joshua and Caleb were in the minority, and their voices were drowned out by the masses who refused to act on God's promise and enter the land. There was one who did hear the two voices: God. In fact, God not only heard the voices of Joshua and Caleb, but also He heard the vehement cries of the majority of the Israelites who spoke against Joshua and Caleb and against the promises of God that had been made known to all. God's judgment came down upon His people because of their outright disobedience to Him. As you know, the Israelites spent forty years wandering in the wilderness until every person of that rebellious generation was dead in the desert. Only two people received the mercy of God which spared them from death in the wilderness and which enabled them to lead the next generation of God's people into the Promised Land. Those two of course were Joshua and Caleb. By the mercies of God, they lived life with conviction and courage and were used by God in a mighty and powerful way to see His purposes fulfilled.

In Romans 12:1 Paul acknowledges that the brethren are to live out this powerful life of worship "by the mercies of God." We must come to the place today where we will cry out before our own generation, much like Joshua and Caleb. We must tackle these problems in Christendom simply because we have no choice and because God requires it of us. Our hearts must be both broken and emboldened as we make a plea before our God asking Him to have mercy upon us, a sinful and wayward people who have failed time and time again in our own strength.

The noted Matthew Henry wrote that the "mercies of God" mentioned by the apostle Paul are "an affectionate obtestation . . . which should melt us into compliance."[7] This obtestation is exactly what happened in the hearts of our leaders at Ridgewood Church where I serve as a pastor. Our hearts were melted with the state of Christendom and the lack of life-changing power in the people in the pews. More specifically, we were sick before the Lord about our children, and we asked for His mercy to help us reclaim our young people.

We saw firsthand the alarming facts about the youth in our churches. In the late nineties, Ridgewood started a Christian school to service our community. During the last ten years, we have seen hundreds of Christian teens come through our doors. We saw these students for more than forty hours a week for thirty-nine weeks each year. Compare this to the time a typical youth minister will see his students, which is approximately three hours a week. The students had attended some of the "best" youth ministries in our area, and yet exhibited a worldly mind-set and lifestyle that was often masked when they attended their own youth ministries at their local churches.

We would see other pastors and youth ministers in town who would talk about the depth of their youth's spirituality, youth who attended our academic institution. We would insist that they must be talking about someone else. We saw firsthand that the national norms of Christian teens' beliefs and lifestyles that were previously mentioned in this chapter were a local norm as well. A serious problem faced us in our own backyards, and people were blind to it. I can attribute only the mercies of God for opening our eyes to the reality around us. The reality hit us hard. It hit us even harder when we examined the history of the youth in our own church.

We are a group of young pastors who have more than forty years of youth and singles' ministry experience between us. We had to confront the reality that our best efforts during these faithful years of service had produced the declared failure rates that were being printed as fast as they were being researched. I remember one staff meeting where we all were challenged with one question, "Will you allow your own children to attend the programs, lock-ins, socials, and camps that you have attended and/or supervised during your years of ministry to youth?" Silence was heard. Tears filled eyes. The consensus was emphatically no. All we could say was, "Lord, have mercy on us and show us *Your* way to lead *Your* people!" We knew something had to be done differently in order to recapture the hearts of our young people for the sake of future generations.

I also remember the time when my dear friend and fellow pastor, Kyle, started to clean up the church's isolated youth room. You see, Kyle was not your typical youth minister. He persevered far beyond the average burnout rate of youth ministry service at one place. Kyle was the youth minister at Ridgewood Church for more than eleven years. He actually saw students enter the youth ministry at sixth-grade level and leave it upon graduation from high school. Kyle saw large numbers in Sunday school and on Wednesday nights and was a part of many late nights at summer camp where kids made the tearful decisions to sell out to Jesus. Kyle even oversaw a large youth room with a built-in stage and colorful, hip youth décor (and let us not forget about the pool table, ping pong table, and the air hockey table that never worked).

The time I recall and recount to you is when Kyle had to clear a sixty-foot youth room wall that was filled with pictures from his eleven years of youth ministry. Tears filled his eyes as one by one Kyle took down pictures that focused on students he knew were not serving the Lord today. Students who were the youth "leaders" and students who had surrendered to missions or the ministry were all part of the casualties. Prison, sexual promiscuity, unwed pregnancies, drug and alcohol abuse, divorce, partying, cutting, participation in the Gothic subculture, and lack of church attendance were common in the lives of approximately three-fourths of the students in the "vibrant" youth ministry of our church.

Of course, there were exceptions of students who were saved and rescued and are living faithful lives to this day. Praise God for His mercy in their lives! But these were the exceptions and not the norm. A 12–30 percent success rate is nothing to brag about. It is definitely not a rate that demonstrates the power of our God! It exposes a huge power loss.

The Appeal Has Been Made to You and Me

"Church, we have a problem" that faces us today. (I'm sorry if I am overusing the Apollo 13 line . . . but we do have a problem.) We can be a church of ostriches and continue to have our heads in the sands of futility, or we can be a church that accepts the admonition from Paul in Romans 12:1 and acts upon His appeal to live lives that are different. Lives that are acceptable and pleasing to Him. Lives that will impact generations to come. The future of Christianity is at stake. The future of our children, grandchildren, and great-grandchildren is in our hands. Will you join me and others in the spirit of Joshua and Caleb and charge forward and conquer the giants among us?

Chapter 2

Run, Run as Fast as You Can!
Rejecting the Secularization of the Church

Do not be conformed to this world. (Romans 12:2a)

During the fall of 2007, I received an encouraging late-night phone call from my former pastor and mentor. He jovially asked me if I had heard what Bill Hybels had said at a recent Summit Leadership conference. I told him I had not, and he went on explaining to me the gist of what was said in order to encourage me and the church to stay the course we were on in spite of the naysayers. So I did what any good twenty-first century individual would do. I immediately Googled "Bill Hybels says they made a mistake." And *voila*! Scores of blogs and articles concerning his statements appeared. After reading a few articles, I went straight to the horse's mouth by watching the actual video of Hybels's message entitled "The Wake-up Call of My Adult Life." (I encourage you to watch this at http://revealnow.com/story.asp?storyid=49.)

Before I go on, let me say a few things about Bill Hybels. First, I do not know the man. Second, I do not presume to question his character. In fact, I have read and immensely enjoyed several of his books and there is no denying he has a passion for lost souls. He is a gifted and wonderful orator. Third, I was more than thrilled to hear his humble recognition of the serious faith crisis that the community of Willow Creek in Chicago and other churches faced; however, as I'll try to explain, I was disappointed at his solution to the problem.

During his message at the conference, Hybels talked about the scientific in-house research that was done by one of his associates at Willow Creek Community Church. The results of the study led Hybels to make the following observation:

> Some of the stuff we have put millions of dollars into thinking it would really help our people grow and develop spiritually, when the data actually came back, it wasn't helping people that much. Other things that we didn't put much money into and didn't put much staff against is stuff our people are crying out for.[1]

He goes on to say, "We made a mistake."[2] His humility was encouraging especially because untold thousands have mimicked Willow's ministry model. He had enough courage to say they had exhausted millions of dollars on programs that have not produced true and lasting fruit for the kingdom of God. I truly admire the man and his character.

You may then ask why I was so disappointed. My hopes were up as I listened to this influential pastor build up his audience for the climax of his message. He had eloquently stated the problem, and now the solution was to be presented. As I was watching my computer screen, I was muttering under my breath, "C'mon, say it. Say it." I wanted him to throw away the marker and board and pick up the Bible. Yes, the Bible. I wanted to hear him say that they have been wrong in all of their humanistic and pragmatic approaches to ministry, and I wanted him to turn to the eternal Book and say, "The answer has been here all along!"

If you have stopped reading this book to watch Hybels's message online, then you already know that this is not what he said. To my bewilderment, he introduced another pragmatic solution to offset the admittedly poor results of thirty years of pragmatic church-growth practices. Here is what he said concerning the beginning of their new plan, just in case you have not watched it yet.

> The leadership team right now, are working very hard on how to *rethink* on how we coach people to full spiritual development and they're taking this into serious consideration. We're *pioneering* this thing called Personal Spiritual Growth Plans. Customized personal spiritual growth plans for everybody at Willow. *You go to a health club and you get a personal trainer who tells you how you can do physical conditioning in the way you need it.* Well, we need to provide customized personal spiritual growth plans to people at Willow to get them to become self-feeders."[3] (emphasis added)

In light of the revelation of their study on their own church and six others that called for people to be self-feeders, do we really need something that is "pioneering" or do we just need to repent of our ways and get back to the tested and proven Bible alone for spiritual growth? Do we need to hijack the system that is currently in place at health clubs to empower people to do their Christian duties, or do we just need to repent and submit ourselves to the power of the indwelling Spirit of God that inhabits true believers?

After all, wasn't it Paul who told Timothy that "all Scripture is breathed out by God and profitable for teaching, for reproof, for correction, and for training in righteousness, that the man of God may be competent, equipped for every good work" (2 Timothy 3:16–17). If Paul said "all" Scripture is all the man of God needs to be competent and equipped for "every" thing he'll be called to do, then why does the modern-day church continue to ride the waves of the latest fads of our culture to run His church? In the next chapter we will discuss the sufficiency of Scripture and how it relates to all that we are and all that we are to do. I do agree with Hybels that Christians need to be self-feeders, but I don't agree that we need to look to the world to see this accomplished.

I know what many of you may be thinking right now, because I have been criticized about this already. *Dustin, aren't you being a little idealistic in our twenty-first century world?* Guilty as charged! Paul said that we are not to be "conformed to this world" in Romans 12:2. And as we have already seen, the lifestyles of Christians in our day are conformed wholeheartedly to the world's ways. Why? It is because our churches operate on the basic principles of the humanistic philosophy of pragmatism and no longer on the unchanging ideals of the Bible. Proverbs 23:7 says that a man is what he thinks in his heart (KJV). So if we are ruled by the thinking of the world, we should not be taken aback to see the majority of churchgoers acting like the world.

In order to recapture the much-needed power and favor of our God, you and I must start with the thinking and mind-set of the people in our churches. To go one step further, you and I must deal with our own thinking and mind-set before we can deal with the thinking of others. So what are we to do? We are to reject unabashedly the secularization of the church and ministry. There is absolutely no lasting and eternal power in the futility of man's thinking and ways which fluctuate daily like the tides of an ocean. Do not be conformed to this world any longer!

The Problem with Pragmatism

First, what is pragmatism? The philosophy of pragmatism in our day was highly influenced by the humanistic educator John Dewey.[4] It is defined by *The Oxford Pocket Dictionary* as "an approach that assesses the truth of meaning of theories or beliefs in terms of the success of their practical application."[5] Since success is the goal no matter the approach, pragmatism simply promotes a the-end-justifies-the-means mentality. Since the end justifies the means, it is our experiences of success or failure that become the standard for future choices. Essentially, our circumstances, which are ever changing, dictate what we are to do in a given situation to produce the desired result in that moment. There are no absolutes in pragmatism, which is why the philosophy of pragmatism has been the precursor to relativism in our culture which basically says that truths are not absolute but are relative to an individual and/or their circumstances.

Okay then. How has pragmatism influenced the church? Pragmatism has led churches to ask the question "Will it work?" instead of asking the question "Is it true and biblical?" Our modern-day church growth movement is not only rooted in pragmatism, it encourages it. Early church growth movement advocate C. Peter Wagner in his 1981 book *Your Church Can Grow* wrote:

> We ought to see clearly that the end DOES justify the means. What else possibly could justify the means? If the method I am using accomplishes the goal I am aiming at, it is for that reason a good method. If, on the other hand, my method is not accomplishing the goal, how can I be justified in continuing to use it?"[6]

Church growth advocates like Wagner don't even hide the fact that "the end justifies the means" is the foundation of their goals of church growth. To be fair to Wagner, he does state that the means should not be ungodly methods. The fact still remains, however, that pragmatism is an accepted philosophy in the church. It is pragmatism that can lead a pastor like Hybels to introduce a plan modeled after health clubs to chart spiritual growth. If the spiritual health plan works for people in the church, then it is a good idea. If it doesn't, then it is back to paper and pen to come up with another plan to implement. When the ABC's of a church's success in our day are Attendance, Buildings, and Cash,[7] it is very easy to succumb to the secular pragmatic approaches of ministry that fill the bookshelves of church-growth sections in our Christian bookstores. Church growth in our day is about numbers at any cost. Sprinkle some sweet biblical principles on an ingenious church-growth plan that will work for you and other churches, then you can sell a few books and speak at the big conferences. The end justifies the means. If the end is good, then the means must be right. The battle cry goes like this, "Bless God! If souls are getting saved, that is all that matters!" Let me inject a quote by Franky Schaeffer from his book *Addicted to Mediocrity* at this point. Schaeffer wrote, "The excuse that 'sometimes people are saved' is no excuse at all. People have been saved in concentration camps because God can bring good from evil, but this does not justify the evil."[8] The institutional church in the West has been conformed to the world.

The Church Has Gone Secular

I must return to the story of our personal plight as church leaders when we came to grips with the seriousness of the crisis we were facing in the local church. We knew there was a problem, and we knew something had to be done. One of the things that the Lord started to reveal to me was the similarity between the way the church educates and disciples our children and the way our world educates and disciples its children. I had to go back and challenge the strongholds that were established in my mind from my own personal educational experience. I have always worked in some capacity with kids since I was fifteen years old. I wanted to have an impact on young people, so it was only natural for me to pursue a career in the educational world. It was the schooling and training I received regarding the mental, behavioral, and physical growth and development of children and adolescents from two pedagogy departments at two different universities that the Lord brought to my memory.

I started seeing that we in the church have actually adopted the world's philosophies in our children's and youth ministries (and in ministry to adults as well, but for time's sake we will focus on children and youth mainly). I started seeing the influences of Horace Mann, G. Stanley Hall, John Dewey, Sigmund Freud, and Carl Jung as well as others (Kant, Darwin, Skinner, Marx, Kierkegaard, Rousseau, etc.). The humanistic natural sciences and philosophies geared toward both understanding and influencing child, youth, and basic human development that I studied in college were now the undergirding philosophy of how we schedule and run our churches on a weekly basis! To say that all of the influential men mentioned (and not mentioned) held to the exact same beliefs or philosophies would be elementary of me. To say that they all share a few common threads with each other would be fair. Most were atheists (or agnostics at best) who in some form or another believed the common good of man would be achieved through socialistic means (such as age segregation and socialization) along with the eradication of religion, Christianity in particular. Regarding age segregation, G. Stanley Hall, often called the "Father of Adolescence" and the "Father of Psychology," was a Darwinian whose 1904 book was a major contributor to age segregation in public schools.[9] Hall's theory of evolutionary recapitulation "contended that children at each age in their development paralleled a particular phase of human evolution, and we should group children accordingly so as not to mix up the evolutionary process."[10]

When it comes to the eradication of Christianity, John Dewey, who is often called the "Father of Modern Education" and the "Father of Modern Pragmatism", was a coauthor of the "Humanist Manifesto I" that said, "There is no God and no soul. Hence there are no needs for the props of traditional religion. With dogma and creed excluded, the immutable truth is also dead and buried. There is no room for fixed, natural law or permanent moral absolutes."[11]

The can of worms I just opened by grouping these secular humanists and philosophers together is much too big to deal with in this chapter. I know this, and I also know that suggesting our churches run off of secular philosophies, psychology, and influences is a much deeper (and much needed) subject to broach. I would speculate, however, that most people in church life have no clue who most of these guys are and have not read many books, if any, that deal with their influence on society and the church. A few books I recommend to get you started on are Francis Schaeffer's classic *How Should We Then Live?*, David Breese's *Seven Men Who Rule the World from the Grave*, David A. Black's *Myth of Adolescence*, John MacArthur's *Think Biblically*, George Barna's *Think Like Jesus*, Tim LaHaye's *Mind Siege*, Chuck Colson and Nancy Pearcey's *How Now Shall We live?*, and John Taylor Gatto's *The Underground History of American Education*.

Our church is located in an area that has a church on every street corner. Name the denomination and we've got it. Name a Baptist denomination and we've got more than we need. We are a Southern Baptist church that has six other Baptist churches in a 2.5 mile radius of us. Having enough churches ain't our problem down here. The Lord really

Turning the Ship

opened my eyes during the beginning stages of turning the ship at our church concerning the plethora of churches around us and across our nation. The eye opener was the thought, *Why do all the churches in our area have the exact same weekly schedule and structure?* No matter the denomination—be it the different Baptists, Methodists, Lutherans, Presbyterians, Episcopalians, Churches of Christ, Disciples of Christ, nondenominational churches, Assemblies of God, charismatic churches, and others—all had a segregated Sunday-school hour followed by a main worship service that had a separate children's church. Most have some sort of segregated children's and youth program on Sunday or Wednesday evenings with many different denominations using the very same curriculum. Much to my surprise, even the Catholic church that I grew up in has adopted some evangelical trends for reaching younger people by offering Vacation Bible School and a "youth" Sunday evening Mass with a praise band.

Adults are not immune to intentional segregation either. The typical church, no matter the denomination, has a senior citizen group, empty nesters, married with older children, married with younger children, married with older and younger children, divorced and remarried, divorced and still single, never-been-married 40-somethings, never-been-married 30-somethings, don't-need-to-be-married-yet 20-somethings, and so on. I was truly floored by this profound revelation of the lack of differences in the models or approaches of our modern-day churches. Often the only differences seemed to be in the church's denominational name, not in the people or their practices.

Why was this so? The answer is that the secular influence on the church at large has shaped how we schedule and program church. Let's deal with one secular and detrimental practice that is used in the modern-day church. If you haven't written me off as a lunatic yet, you probably will when we briefly tackle the sacred cows of church nursery and children's church. (In case of hyperventilation, I heard you are to breathe in a paper bag. In case of outright fury, I heard you are to breathe in a plastic bag. Please smile!)

One of the beauties of age-integrated churches is that children are welcome in the gathering of the body of Christ and do not at any time go to a designated children's church. People's first reaction to having cooing babies and children in the church gathering is rooted in selfishness. Unfortunately, since we are influenced by secularism, the world naturally revolves around us and our experiences. Adult churchgoers act like consumers and treat the church service like they are in an airplane or a movie theater where they do not want any disruptive kid ruining their experience. So the stewardesses, I mean ushers, politely tell guests and members that they have a nursery available in the back and a children's church that starts when the preacher gets up to preach.

And don't you just love how we sugarcoat getting children out of the service with spiritual reasoning and justification like, "I don't get anything out of the service if a kid is acting up during church." And the super spiritual will say, "*Others* will not get anything out of the service if a kid is acting up during church." Recently my family and I went to a Christmas concert at a *USA Today* top-50 church north of Houston. I have a habit of collecting bulletins at churches I attend, so I naturally picked up the bulletin for the weekend service to be held. This church was creative in its marketing. In the bulletin it had a classy smiling picture of the pastor and his wife with a greeting that told people to take advantage of their exciting children's ministry by sending their children to another part of the campus so everyone could get the most out of their experience in the main service. Why can't people just be honest and say, "NO KIDS ALLOWED!"? About the same time of the season, a family from our church visited a church's Christmas pageant in our area where they were offended when a pastor greeted the large crowd by jokingly, yet seriously, encouraging people to "make sure you put your children on vibrate and take your cell phones to the nursery." What was most disheartening was that the Christian-filled crowd laughed at this twisted humor. God help us!

Most people in the church pews and most church-growth gurus and leaders are now more educated and dignified than ever. They have matured well beyond the spiritual reasons why children need to be cut off from the body. In their puffed-up explanations they say, "Children's church is for the well-being of the children because the church has trained professionals that know how to teach children in a way that best suits the developmental stage that they are in." They say it actually would be of no benefit for the children to sit in big church. They make superior enlightened comments. "Kids need to learn on their level." "Kids learn best with children their own age." "The preacher's message would be over the heads of these children." "Kids learn best when they are active and involved with hands-on learning." "Kids would be bored in big church." "We must think about the children and their enjoyment." "If we don't teach, then who will? Their parents won't do it and even if they could, they aren't qualified to do it." On and on it goes. All of these educated excuses (and any other ones you can come up with) are purely secular and not biblical. The next chapter will actually deal with the biblical arguments in favor of having children in the main gathering, or big church. But staying right now with the secular, I want to briefly cite from the 1965 secular textbook *The Developing Child*. This is a book I used as a resource back in my pedagogy studies. (Be very thankful that I sold my actual college textbooks at the end of each semester to get a little bit of money or you would have a lot more citations coming at you.) I want to quote a long section and emphasize certain words or phrases with italics. Your intellectual job is to take these comments and see which ones of the above-enlightened quotations in favor of children's church actually parallel this secular garbage.

Childhood *"Revisited"*: Childhood *Discovered*— Because a *surge* in the study of children and an interest in their behavior *have developed in the past few generations,* our era is often called the *"century of the child." For the first time, researchers and scholars developed* the *tools* and the *methods* to study child growth and development *scientifically. One discovery led to the next until, today,* centers for child study exist all over the world. *Thousands of books and articles about children* are published each year; *religious advisors, physicians, psychologists, social workers, and teachers* devote their energies to studying children and helping them lead a richer life. The fact that you as students are studying and learning about children reveals the importance now attached to their understanding and guidance. *Check with your mother or grandmother. Did she study units or courses such as this?*

One result of such interest and activity is that many of the reasons underlying growth and behavior have been—and continue to be—*discovered*. Today, *experts* can make sound recommendations for children's care. *No longer are such suggestions a whim of the times or the pronouncement of the village "wise man"* . . . Following heightened *awareness* of children's physical development, *near the beginning of our century,* came appreciation of their intellectual and emotional growth . . . In Austria, *Sigmund Freud* arrived at the *startling conclusion* that the emotional experiences of childhood indelibly mark the adult personality. *These and other discoveries routed forever the centuries-encrusted notion* that children are merely miniature adults. Instead, they began to be respected as individuals with *separate,* distinct traits and patterns of growth and development which were, nevertheless, *closely related to the years that followed.* Perhaps the relationship between childhood and the adult years is best expressed by the poet William Wordsworth, who wrote: '*The child is father of the man.*' Think about what that means." (italics added)[12]

This is only the tip of the iceberg in this school textbook. You either smell the garbage in that passage or you don't, and just because someone in church life can't smell it doesn't mean it doesn't stink. The Bible, parents, and pastors were all undermined in the above quote. Sorrowfully, the modern-day church develops its children's and youth programs and curriculums off of these new and enlightened secular "discoveries." Recently I received a twenty-plus-page resource catalog promoting the children's Sunday-school curriculum offered by my denomination's resource entity, and it mirrored the stuff propagated in the above secular textbook and the thousands like it. There was not one Scripture verse or reference in the whole catalog; rather it explained why each level was geared specifically to meet the developmental needs of each segregated age group. Don't you know that as a father of a special-needs child, my heart was elated to see that they have a special program geared just for these special kids! (Again I have drifted into sarcasm with that last statement, but I hope you see the church has gone secular.)

Immediately when you talk of doing away with children's church or youth church or just trying to integrate all generations together, the ugly head of pragmatism once again will rise up and speak. The pragmatic monster spoke early on in our transition when we did away with our Wednesday night youth and children's programs in order for the church to gather and worship together as a whole. At this time it must be noted that we still had youth and children's programs for Sunday morning Sunday school and Sunday night discipleship, so we were just talking about integrating one hour out of three a week. No big deal, right? Not to some of the youth. You would have thought both their momma and dog had died. Several made comments that they would never come back again if they had to be with the older people and little kids. Monster Pragmatism would taunt us and say, "We are going to lose all of our young people if we don't offer something just for them!" The Lord quickly slew that pragmatic lie by revealing that we never had those young people to begin with. What the Lord uncovered was that we, the church and our segregated programs, were actually fostering sinful young hearts that were selfish, disobedient, and rebellious against any and all authority. The thing that breaks my heart is to hear the monster of pragmatism speak through the lips of church leaders of our day. They use the same argument against biblical age integration that unregenerate young people spoke against us and our church. "They won't come unless we have something just for them." "If we don't reach them, who will?!" Sorry to say, but they are not being reached right now, and many salvations must be called into question because of the power loss in their lives. "But, but, but, this kid or that kid in my ministry wouldn't be where they are today if . . ." You may be right. Thank God that He moves in the hearts of His children in spite of us. Thank God that in His mercy our failure rate is only 12–30 percentage points away from being 100 percent failure.

Run, Run, as Fast as You Can!

Paul says that we are not to conform to this world. We must take this at face value and reject any high and lofty argument that presents itself against our God and His Word.

(See 2 Corinthians 10:3–5.) We must rid our churches of programs that mirror the vain and empty philosophies of this world. (See Colossians 2:8.) We must be willing to expose the darkness by bringing things to light because the days are evil. (See Ephesians 5:11.)

At Ridgewood, we were truly humbled by the Lord when He exposed a lot of our false thinking as church leaders. We started sharing our story with the people. We challenged their thinking and mind-sets. We laid out the challenge to become a biblically literate people who operate from a biblical worldview. Tackling biblical illiteracy and constructing a biblical framework from which to live were the beginnings of a whole new world for our church. It is amazing how much of the world's ways in us will be exposed when we simply delve wholeheartedly into the Word.

As I close this chapter, I just hope some sense was made in just a few short pages. I hope you have the desire to reject the secularization of ministry. If no desire is present, then you may be one who will be writing off the idea that the church has become secularized. Or maybe your prosperity and success is because of the pragmatic approaches of our obsessed church-growth culture, and so in your mind, it works for you (pragmatically speaking of course). If so, I want to leave you with one more warning of where pragmatism will ultimately lead.

The warning comes from the children's story that I read to my girls called *The Gingerbread Man*. I'm sure you've heard of it. If you can recall, the gingerbread man was very confident in his abilities to outwit and outrun everyone else. He proved his abilities by successfully outrunning those who would have loved to eat him. You always knew when reading the story that one day the continued success of the gingerbread man would be his downfall. He kept running away from those who wanted to snack on him while yelling the taunting words, "Run, run, as fast as you can. You can't catch me . . . I'm the gingerbread man."[13] He succeeded in outrunning the boy, the man, the woman, the three farmers, the bear, and the wolf. Ah, but there was the sly fox who was dressed up as an old man and who would resort to anything to eat the gingerbread man. Disguised as an old man, the fox tricked our little cookie friend into coming ever so close acting as if he, the fox, were deaf. The gingerbread man, who now because of his previous successes thought he was immune to failure, was swallowed up by the fox. The moral of the story is that sometimes in our church lives we rely on our own strengths and past successes to keep on running away from the evil one who wants to have us for lunch. No doubt that we have to keep running for the sake of the gospel. But often it is our perceived success that blinds us with willful arrogance that will ultimately lead us, or our children, or even our children's children to be devoured by the cunning fox, I mean world.

Paul tells us not to be conformed to this world. His call is for us to run as fast as we can from the secularization of ministry. However, even in our running we must not rely on the cunning of man, rather we are to rely upon the sufficiency of an all-sufficient Savior and His Word. Not only do we have something to run from, we humbly have Someone to run to.

Chapter 3

Humpty Dumpty Has Been Made Whole!
Relying on the Sufficiency of Scripture

Be transformed by the renewal of your mind.
(Romans 12:2b)

I turn from one children's story to another. This one is the nursery rhyme of "Humpty Dumpty." Say it with me:

"Humpty Dumpty sat on a wall;
Humpty Dumpty had a great fall.
All the king's horses and all the king's men
couldn't put Humpty together again!"

In keeping with what has been written thus far, the fallen and shattered state of Humpty Dumpty represents the seriousness of the crisis that confronts us in Christianity. The fact that the very best men the king had to offer could not salvage poor Humpty embodies the futility of pragmatism and human efforts that tirelessly try to put Christianity and the church back in working order.

For the secular humanist, the story ends with Humpty lying there broken and splattered and without hope. And sadly, to some in the church, all may seem lost and without hope for the future of Christianity. They see a lackluster church that is having little or no impact on our culture. They see a church that is broken and is completely exposed to the watching eyes of a scoffing world. They may even have as many of the pragmatic church growth books on their shelves as I have in my study, yet they find themselves hopelessly saying, "I've been there and done that and still we seem to be losing the battle."

I would challenge and encourage you that it is high time to quit looking to the "kings" of this world for a quick patch job; instead, we are to look to the One who is the King of Kings and has the ability to make both a person and His people completely whole. Jesus Christ, the author and finisher of our faith, is the only one who can salvage what we in the church have messed up. There is indeed hope for Christians today who desire to see the faith restored to the young people of our day and to the generations of tomorrow.

Transforming Power That Saves

In Romans 12:2 Paul calls all believers to be transformed. This transformation happens by the renewing of our minds. You can easily decipher that the positive aspect of being transformed is in direct contrast to being conformed to this world. Hence, we can logically conclude that there is nothing in the world that can bring about the supernatural transformation that Paul calls for in Romans 12. We can also logically conclude from the text that it is only those who are called "the brethren" in Christ Jesus who can have the ability to have their minds transformed.

We must turn to another passage of Scripture to shed light on why only those who are truly the "brethren" can have this mind renewal Paul is talking about. Paul tells the believers at the church of Corinth that they (true believers) have been given the mind of Christ. He paints the stark contrast between the wisdom of God and the wisdom of men and states that only those who are of the Spirit can even ascertain the wisdom of God. Earthly men, void of the Spirit, are spiritually blinded and unable to understand. Read for yourself.

> Now we have received not the spirit of the world, but the Spirit who is from God, that we might understand the things freely given us by God. And we impart this in words not taught by human wisdom but taught by the Spirit, interpreting spiritual truths to those who are spiritual. The natural person does not accept the things of the Spirit of God, for they are folly to him, and he is not able to understand them because they are spiritually discerned. The spiritual person judges all things, but is himself to be judged by no one. "For who has understood the mind of the Lord so as to instruct him?" But we have the mind of Christ. (1 Corinthians 2:12–16)

It is those who have received the Spirit who have the mind of Christ. When a person is supernaturally transformed by the Spirit of God in the act of regeneration, they are given the mind of Christ. They have been "born again" and made "new creatures in Christ" apart from any human "works" or deeds. (See John 3:3, 2 Corinthians 5:17, Ephesians 2:8–9, Titus 3:5). By repenting and placing their faith in Jesus Christ alone for salvation, true followers of Christ are supernaturally transformed! The Creator of the universe supernaturally invades His natural created world to save stone-hearted sinners. He says, "I will give them one heart, and a new spirit I will put within them. I will remove the heart of stone from their flesh and give them a heart of flesh, that they may walk in my statutes and keep my rules and obey them. And they shall be my people, and I will be their God" (Ezekiel 11:19–20).

When we go back to Romans 12:2 and talk about having minds renewed, we must agree that only those whose minds have been made "new" in the first place through salvation in Jesus Christ can then have their minds "renewed" as they are continually transformed into the image of Christ Himself. The sixteenth-century reformer, John Calvin, said in his commentary of Romans "that every man must be born again, who would enter into the Kingdom of God; for in the mind and heart we are altogether alienated from the righteousness of God."[1] One cannot heed Paul's admonition without first accepting the gospel invitation to salvation.

Transforming Power That Renews

We have just defined that Christians can only be transformed by the renewing of their minds if they are truly Christians who have been transformed by being born again, thus receiving the mind of Christ. We move forward now with the acceptance that the mind of Christ is forever in place in those who believe, and we must look at how believers are to live out Paul's instruction of being transformed by the renewing of their minds as they reject conformity to this world (of course while returning to the emphasis on age-integration in the church).

In order for believers to have their minds renewed, there must be a standard to base their renewal on. I hope you have come to the conclusion that the standard cannot be found in the futility of the world's knowledge. The transformation of the mind Paul is talking about can only be set against the unchanging rule of the Bible. A believer's mind can only be renewed by the Word of God. This should come as no surprise for just two chapters earlier in the book of Romans, we read that it is through the proclamation of the Word of God that people are transformed supernaturally in salvation because "faith comes from hearing, and hearing through the word of Christ" (Romans 10:17).

The same powerful words that usher in new life through salvation are the same powerful words that bring about mind renewal which in turn brings about a life that is pleasing to God. The guidebook has been written. The Bible is the standard by which we are to conduct ourselves in our individual Christian walk and in our collective walk together as the church.

I mentioned earlier that I was raised Roman Catholic. I did not start reading the Bible until I was a freshman in college. The Bible opened up a whole new world to me! To say that prior to that time I didn't believe the Bible would be wrong. I was a good Catholic boy, and although I was never encouraged to read the Bible, I was taught to respect it. Sure I believed the Bible. I just didn't know what the Bible said.

When I entered into the Baptist world, I was so excited because here was a group of people who not only said they believed the Bible, they carried it with them and didn't have to use the index to find anything in it. But much to my disappointment, I would soon discover that aside from a handful of popular Bible verses and a few popular Old Testament stories, the majority of Baptist believers really didn't know what they believed and why when they were pressed. Sure Baptists believed the Bible. Many just didn't know what it said.

But the Bible was the centerpiece of Baptist church life. It was brought to church by attendees, and it was claimed to be the source of the preacher's message. It was the purported basis of all programs for kids, youth, and adults. Baptists were proud to be people of the Book. But one thing always bothered me. Often the preacher or others would spit and holler that they believed that the Bible was inerrant and infallible (to which I say, "Amen!"), but their message or sermon would not systematically deal with the Bible. They would read a Scripture passage once and not return to it until they tried to wrap up their message. My troubled question was, "If they keep saying the Bible is God's Word, why is it rarely used in the sermon?" That question over the years has evolved into, "If they keep saying the Bible is God's Word, why is it rarely used in the practice and operation of the church?"

For years this perplexed me, and I would get into discussions and preach messages that tried to properly explain the problem before us. I finally heard a clear and succinct explanation of the problem and the simple solution. I attended a youth minister's forum that was held at Southwestern Baptist Seminary and sponsored by the Southern Baptists of Texas Convention. The sole reason for this conference was to respond to the dire crisis that the church faces, particularly with our young people. They had eight panelists who are well respected in youth-ministry circles. Each panelist had a fifteen-minute opportunity to address the problem and offer solutions before they engaged in a panel discussion. All eight panelists did a fine job, and the conference was by no means dull. Several of the speakers were plagued by the big *but* syndrome. (Did I mention that I would discuss that sickness later?) These speakers kept my troubled theory alive. Dr. Voddie Baucham finally spoke to the problem I was having but didn't quite know how to articulate. He mentioned in his solo segment that they at his church believed not only in the inerrancy of Scripture, but also the sufficiency of Scripture.[2] He stressed this point twice in his short time. It was not until the panel discussion that his emphasis on believing in the sufficiency of Scripture exposed the fallacy of the pragmatic, secular thinking that gives lip service to believing the Bible is inerrant but not living like it truly is.

During the panel discussion, Dr. Baucham and another guest got into a verbal exchange concerning Christian education. Dr. Baucham used a myriad of Scripture texts and references to defend his argument while the other gentleman used personal experiences and other anecdotes to argue his side. Dr. Baucham challenged the panelist to give him one Scripture that supported his point. After several challenges to produce Scripture, the panelist finally gave one. Dr. Baucham looked at the text in context and hit it right back to the panelist saying that the text actually supported his, Dr. Baucham's, point instead of the panelist's who tossed it up.

Here's the clincher. The only argument the flustered panelist could respond with was that the text from the gospel was written to an agrarian society implying that the text does not apply to the current culture of twenty-first-century America. Dr. Baucham, at this juncture, restated the thesis of his earlier presentation by saying that is exactly why he has been stating that they (he and his church) believe not only in the inerrancy of Scripture, but also the sufficiency. Case closed, right? You would think, but I am sad to say that for whatever reason, the truth of his statement seemed to go right over the enlightened heads of some of the other panelists.

But for me, his words were an invigorating breath of fresh air that only confirmed what the Lord was doing at Ridgewood as we were slowly turning the ship of His church desiring to have the Bible alone as our guide.

The church at large must rely on the sufficiency of Scripture as it is God's divine map and blueprint to keep His body pure and on course. The word *sufficiency* simply means that something is sufficient. *Webster's* defines *sufficient* as having as much as needed or desired.[3] If something is sufficient, there is nothing else needed beyond the very thing that is sufficient. It is not only enough, it is more than enough. So if anyone says that the Scripture is sufficient, they are simply saying that the Bible has everything that we will ever need to live the life God has called us to live. The Bible is not only enough, it is more than enough!

Pastor and author John McArthur in his book *How to Get the Most Out of God's Words* plainly says, "The Bible is sufficient. Because the Word of God is the breath of God, and we don't need anything more."[4] The apostle Peter said it like this:

> For we did not follow cleverly devised myths when we made known to you the power and coming of our Lord Jesus Christ . . . And we have something more sure, the prophetic word, to which you will do well to pay attention as to a lamp shining in a dark place, until the day dawns and the morning star rises in your hearts, knowing this first of all, that no prophecy of Scripture comes from someone's own interpretation. For no prophecy was ever produced by the will of man, but men spoke from God as they were carried along by the Holy Spirit. (2 Peter 1:16a, 19–21)

The apostle Paul said it like this:

> All Scripture is breathed out by God and profitable for teaching, for reproof, for correction, and for training in righteousness, that the man of God may be competent, equipped for every good work. (2 Timothy 3:16–17)

The Lord Jesus Christ said it like this:

> For truly, I say to you, until heaven and earth pass away, not an iota, not a dot, will pass from the Law until all is accomplished. Therefore, whoever relaxes one of the least of these commandments and

teaches others to do the same will be called least in the kingdom of heaven, but whoever does them and teaches them will be called great in the kingdom of heaven. (Matthew 5:18–19)

Now, what do you say? What does the church at large say? I say that the Bible is sufficient for all matters of faith and practice and that it transcends all cultures and all times. Will you join me in standing with some pretty good company (Jesus, Peter, and Paul), who thought pretty highly of God's Word, and help turn the church around and pursue biblical integrity and fidelity?

The Sufficiency of Scripture for Having Children in the Gathering

Finally, we have arrived together to what many have wanted me to get to since the last chapter. Why should children attend "big church"? What is wrong with children's church? (Please remember, I am only using children's church as one example of a church practice that is secular and not biblical. There are others that go way beyond the scope of children and youth. Age integration in the church is simply about being the church, and that encompasses everybody of all ages and backgrounds.)

I introduced in the previous chapter that I believe the basis for children's church is purely secular. I'm sure you got that. Now, I want to turn to the positive aspect of having children worshipping with the whole body of Christ from start to finish when the body gathers. In order to do that, we must turn to several Bible passages and trust that Scripture is sufficient for this heated topic. It is clear in the Bible, through both actual events and implication, that children were present when God's people gathered. Let's first journey together to the Old Testament and see this practiced among God's people.

Our first stop is in the book of Deuteronomy. In chapter 31 of Deuteronomy, we have the Lord giving His instructions to Israel through His servant Moses for the last time. The days of the wilderness period are at their end, and the transfer of leadership from Moses to Joshua is taking place. Moses gave the Law to the priests and to the elders and left them with the following details:

> At the end of every seven years, at the set time in the year of release, at the Feast of Booths, when all Israel comes to appear before the LORD your God at the place that he will choose, you shall read this law before *all* Israel in their hearing. *Assemble the people, men, women, and little ones,* and the sojourner within your towns, that *they* may hear and learn to fear the LORD your God, and be careful to do all the words of this law, and that their *children,* who have not known it, may hear and learn to fear the LORD your God, as long as you live in the land that you are going over the Jordan to possess. (Deuteronomy 31:10–13, italics added)

It is clear that children were a part of this general gathering of the Israelite nation to hear the Law of God read. God thought His own Word was important enough and relevant even for children to hear. About the importance of children hearing the Word in this assembly, Matthew Henry wrote, "Note, It is the will of God that all people should acquaint themselves with his word. It is a rule to all, and therefore should be read to all."[5]

This instance of having children in the presence of reading the Law debunks the secular notion that children need to learn on their level in a separate children's church.

Based on the biblical precedent established in Deuteronomy, having children separated from the main gathering of the church body and receiving watered-down instruction in children's church from people who may not even be scripturally qualified to teach is wrong. Are we to neglect our children from the admonition of the Word of God as preached to the body by one of the church's appointed pastors or elders? I love that Matthew Henry said, "It is a rule to all and should be read to all."[6]

In the next chapter, I'll list some personal testimonies of people's experiences with children in our services. Oh and one more thing before we go to the next example. Have you ever read the Law? It is easy for an adult to get bogged down in the Law, but God wanted even children to be in the presence of the public reading of the Law. Yup. God must not think our children are as dumb as we are.

The next biblical event where children were in the presence of the general assembly can be found in Ezra 10. Now, this example discredits the selfish secular church mind-set that says children in a service will disrupt the adults and somehow prevent God from moving in the midst of His people. Ezra was used by God to restore the sinful nation of Israel back to God. A national mourning and confession broke out as the Lord revealed the Israelites' neglect of His Word and their pagan ways such as allowing their children to intermarry with pagans. (Somebody shout, "Stay there a while!") The point for us to make is found in Ezra 10:1. It says, "While Ezra prayed and made confession, weeping and casting himself down before the house of God, a very great *assembly* of men, women, and *children,* gathered to him out of Israel, for the people wept bitterly" (italics added). Children were a part of a great national revival. They didn't hinder anyone's experience on that day.

The first argument that will be made against these two examples is, "That was all Old Testament. We are the New

Testament now." But let's embrace that theologically shallow and liberal challenge by looking in the New Testament. I will be the first one to agree that in the New Testament there are no specific instances such as we read in the Old Testament that list children in the presence of the gathering of the early church. There are several passages that imply that children were in the main gathering and one account that states children were permitted to be in the Lord's presence.

First, one can logically assume that when the early church met in homes and ate together that children were present. Second, we know that many of the epistles we now read in our Bibles were handwritten letters that were to be read publicly to the specified church or churches. For example, the book of Romans was a letter written by Paul to the Church at Rome. This is important to note because we have two letters to churches that have in them specific instructions that were written to children. In Ephesians 6:1–4, children are told to obey their parents and are told why they are to do such a thing. The same admonition for children to obey their parents is found in Colossians 3:20. Both of these letters would have been read by the church at large respectively in Ephesus and Colosse. The instructions for the children in both cases are no different than any of the other commands or instructions written to the adult hearers, be they men or women. It can strongly, therefore, be suggested that children were in the presence of the gatherings of the early church in the New Testament. (A side note: we have no recorded letters written to children's or youth church. Maybe archeologists haven't discovered them yet or maybe they didn't have VeggieTales or puppets back then.)

Probably one of the biggest indictments against the modern-day church for ridding themselves of children in their gatherings comes from the lips of Jesus Christ Himself. In the synoptic gospels we have accounts of Jesus encouraging children to come to Him. It is the account in the gospel of Mark that I want us to look at closely. It reads:

> They were bringing children to him that he might touch them, and the disciples rebuked them. But when Jesus saw it, he was indignant and said to them, "Let the children come to me; do not hinder them, for to such belongs the kingdom of God. Truly, I say to you, whoever does not receive the kingdom of God like a child shall not enter it." And he took them in his arms and blessed them, laying his hands on them. (Mark 10:13–16)

The indictment that I believe can be applied to the modern church is the same indictment of displeasure that Jesus made toward His disciples concerning their keeping children out of His presence. Why were the disciples so adamant in stopping the children and keeping them separated from Jesus? We don't exactly know. It doesn't say. We can conjecture that they saw the children as unworthy nuisances that had no business infringing on their time with Jesus. People haven't changed much, have they?

What I want to bring to our attention is twofold. First, look at how Jesus responded to the attitude of His disciples. The Scripture said Jesus was "indignant" (Mark 10:14) at what He saw. Jesus was angry at the disciples. Although we cannot equate Jesus' righteous anger with the unrighteous anger that Jesus' detractors had against Him, it must be noted that the same word used in Mark 10 to describe Jesus' emotion was the same word used to describe the attitudes of the chief priests and scribes toward the crowd's calling Jesus the Son of David. Matthew 21:15 says, "When the chief priests and the scribes saw the wonderful things that he did, and the children crying out in the temple, 'Hosanna to the Son of David!' they were indignant." It is also very peculiar to note that the chief priests and scribes were "indignant" at children. Jesus rebuked their disregard of the children's praise when He answered the religious leaders by saying, "Yes; have you never read, 'Out of the mouth of infants and nursing babies you have prepared praise'?" (Matthew 21:16).

This last statement by Jesus brings me to the second point I want to make about the account in Mark 10. Look how Jesus responded to children. He loved them. He welcomed them. He hugged them. He blessed them. He said the kingdom belonged to them. He said adults must be like them in order to enter into His kingdom. "Truly, I say to you, unless you turn and become like children, you will never enter the kingdom of heaven. Whoever humbles himself like this child is the greatest in the kingdom of heaven" (Matthew 18:3–4).

This is when someone chimes in and says that "the reason we have children's church is because we *do* love children!" Let me ask a question. Is it generally the typical church's main prayer each Sunday morning that they want "Jesus to be in their presence" or they want to "experience Jesus" or to see "Jesus move in a mighty way"? If those are the prayers of the people in big church, then I would argue that children are not being loved when they are kept away from the very One whom the church gathered to meet.

If we are going to say that the Bible is sufficient, then the facts are clear concerning children's church. There is no biblical argument for having a segregated children's church. Any argument, albeit "spiritual," is pragmatic and is rooted in secular humanism. The church in no way is to usurp the role of parents in the training of their own children. Children need to be with their parents, and children at church without parents need to be under the care of a godly family in order for the biblical family unit to be modeled for them. Jesus loves children, and they are to be welcome in the gathering.

Sola Scriptura

Let us not forget the main point of this chapter. Paul calls for believers to be transformed by the renewing of their minds, and that renewing can only happen when we look to the Bible alone for all knowledge and wisdom. The Bible is sufficient for us in every matter. There is nothing that we as Christians or churches will go through that the Bible is not more than we need to get us through. God is looking for people in Christendom to step up and sound the alarm against the abuses of the modern-day church much like the sixteenth-century reformers did. The battle cry of *sola scriptura,* by Scripture alone, needs to echo from the walls of our churches.

The great news is that God desires to make His people whole and complete if we will humbly turn to Him and His eternal Word in order to "destroy arguments and every lofty opinion raised against the knowledge of God, and take every thought captive to obey Christ, being ready to punish every disobedience, when your obedience is *complete*" (2 Corinthians 10:5–7, italics added).

Chapter 4

The Lights Are Back On!
Recapturing Hearts, Minds, and Souls

That by testing you may discern what is the will of God, what is good and acceptable and perfect. (Romans 12:2b)

I remember the one-year anniversary of my being pastor of Ridgewood Church in Port Arthur, Texas, very well. The reason I remember it so well is that the church did not even gather on the Sunday that marked the anniversary. I didn't receive any cards, and in fact it never crossed anyone's mind. Now before you go and start thinking the worst, you need to understand that my one-year anniversary as lead pastor at Ridgewood was to be celebrated on Sunday, September 25, 2005. So what? The "what" is that on Saturday, September 24, 2005, Hurricane Rita made landfall in Southeast Texas and Southwest Louisiana. There was no church on that Sunday, or the next four to follow, because there was no one in town! Everyone had evacuated.

Our area was hit hard. My family eventually ended up at a duck camp in Monroe, Louisiana, where they stayed for fifteen days. (The long story of how we ended up at a premier duck camp with nice lodging is a God story too long for this book.) I also said they, my family, stayed in Monroe for fifteen days because I came home early. Our church was the living quarters for the Southern Baptist Disaster Relief Team, so I was able to return a few days after the storm while the area was still on government lockdown. The area was devastated. It was unlivable. Electricity was completely lost and was estimated not to be restored for weeks and possibly months.

I remember a time when the emotion of it all caught up with me and overwhelmed me. After a long, hot day of helping with the meal and ice lines which had served the basic three meals to thousands earlier that day, I was finally free to eat. This was a Wednesday night, and I was eating out of a Styrofoam to-go plate on a chair in the church parking lot. I couldn't hold in my emotions anymore. The strangest feeling came over me. I was physically home, but it didn't feel like home. My house was unlivable. No cars were on the highway in front of the church. The church was empty on a Wednesday night. My wife and other family members were still back in Monroe five hours away. I was eating with strangers (godly brothers and sisters thankfully), and nothing was the same. There were only a few more minutes of daylight left before total darkness and mosquitoes would engulf the night sky and area. On top of all this, my wife had just called to tell me the great news that we were being chosen to adopt two little girls, and it would happen in a matter of weeks. So all I could do in that moment was sit there with plastic fork in hand and cry like a little three-year-old girl in the parking lot of our deserted and battered church. Those days were long, lonely, and sometimes even eerie. You just knew that each day that passed meant you were one day closer to normalcy. The Lord and I got pretty close during those days!

Day fourteen rolled around and out of the blue it was like God spoke and the lights came on! I remember calling my wife and saying, "Honey, the lights are on!" On day fifteen my beautiful wife was home to help me clean our house which was only half livable and had to house two new additions in just two short weeks.

I cannot begin to describe to you the enthusiasm and excitement that we experienced when the lights came back on. It was truly unforgettable. Life started coming back when the lights came on. Even though the road to recovery was only beginning, at least now with electricity back on we could see the road we were traveling. Although I thank God for all that He taught me, my family, our church, and the community, I can safely speak for all and say we never want to go back to those days or anything like them.

As we turn the focus back to this book and turning the ship to travel against the current of the church culture of our day, I can say that ever since the lights have come on in the households that make up our church, we have had the resolve never to go back to the way things were done before. I'm no longer talking about Hurricane Rita and the power restoration to our area. I'm talking about the power restoration to the lives of the people who make up the church at Ridgewood. We have come so far in this journey that we can't turn back now, and even if we could, we would not. The lights have been turned on! In much the same way that power was incrementally restored to the homes after Hurricane Rita, so too the Lord has slowly, but faithfully, turned on one light at a time.

I have been addressing the issue of children's church not because getting rid of it is all there is to age integration in the church. It surely is not. I have used it as an example, because if a light does not go off there and if a church can't simply have the whole church worship together, then the subsequent blessings and illumination in other areas of the church concerning age integration won't occur. With that said, I want to bring up children's church one more time as we wrap up part 1 of this book by talking about the powerful experience of bringing children into our main Sunday morning gathering.

As we look at some examples, we need first to refer back to Romans 12:1–2. The last part, referring to the power-filled transformed life which comes about by the renewal of the mind, states that "by testing you may discern what is the will of God, what is good and acceptable and perfect" (Romans 12:2). As we have accepted the appeal to restore power to the church by rejecting the secularization of ministry and by relying on the sufficiency of Scripture, God has no doubt proved Himself by supernaturally turning the lights on in the lives of His children.

The Lights Were Turned On in Our Children's Hearts and Minds

As stated earlier, one of the objections to having children in the main gathering of the church is that everything, especially the sermon, will be over their heads. By speaking against that argument, I am not saying that they will understand with the highest level of comprehension everything that is done or said in big church. Does every adult completely understand fully all that is said and done either? The issue is not trusting in man's comprehensive abilities in church. It is, rather, trusting that the Holy Spirit will teach and touch each individual, no matter what his or her age or intellect, according to God's plan and in His time. God has blown away our finite little minds at Ridgewood by what He has powerfully and supernaturally taught our children ever since they have been worshipping with the whole church.

I recall one mom approaching me and telling me what her seven-year-old daughter asked her while I was preaching: "Mom, what does 'die to yourself' mean?" I can tell you stories of families having their young children ask questions about things that were said in the sermon while they were driving in their cars going home from church. The crazy thing about some of these deep questions is that often the children heard the sermon better than the adults.

Children have actually responded verbally during the sermons to what was being said. Pastor Kyle's two-year-old actually threw me a curve and made me speechless one time when he responded out loud. We were going through the gospel of John, and we stayed in one passage for three weeks. Because of staying in the same text and theme, I used the same PowerPoint background, simply changing the points each week. Well, on week three when I was about to preach, I heard this loud squealing voice coming forth out of the congregation saying, "Not this again!" Not exactly what you want to hear right before you preach. The barely understandable two-year-old (although he spoke plainly on this occasion . . . maybe it was the gift of tongues) recognized the PowerPoint background as being the same from the last two weeks. In other instances when "Amen?" has been said by the one preaching, "Amen!" has come forth from toddlers in the crowd.

I can't tell you the joy I have when either on Saturday night or early Sunday morning my girls will ask me, "Dad, are we going to be in John today?" or whatever other book we are expounding at church. My middle daughter had just turned two years old early on in the process of having no children's church when she floored me with something she said. I was changing her diaper while she was holding a small Precious Moments Bible in her hands. She asked, "Daddy, can you find Colossians for me?" I would have won any Bible sword drill that night! Nobody could have found Colossians faster than I did. Why did she ask that? She heard her daddy every week tell the church to open to the book of Colossians as we all journeyed together through that wonderful epistle verse by verse.

I could go on and on not only about examples of how children in the main gathering picked up things from the sermon, but also how the children of the church light up to sing Christ-exalting music. Just recently, the young ladies of our church, ranging from the age of two to eighteen, led the congregation in worship by singing and signing "Father, We Adore You" and "Holy, Holy, Holy"! The floodlights came on that day!

The Lights Have Been Turned On in Our Children's Souls

Another objection to having children in the main church service is that they can't keep still and they will disturb others. If you were to come to our gathering, you would no doubt hear and see the presence of children. It would be music to your ears. You would find that children are respectful, well behaved, and if they act up, parents are simply encouraged to be parents. Who cares if a parent has to get up to leave the gathering to spank his temper-tantrum kid during the service? There is not a better deterrent in the world for the other children to behave than the screaming kid who leaves to attend a meeting in the bathroom. I am appalled that some churches have signs up telling anyone who would leave their auditorium during the production, I mean service, not to enter back in or not to return to their original seat if it was up in the front.

An amazing thing happens when children are with their parents in big church. Children are trained to display character traits like self-control, patience, and respect. They are taught to obey their parents. "What about the bad kids?" Glad you asked. If someone has unruly kids in the church pew, they have unruly kids at home. Those same unruly kids, if put in a children's church, would be causing the children's church workers Sunday morning frustration, while their parents sit and try to relax long enough to get something out of the message. And just when the parents' flustered minds are starting to clear up, a restaurant-style pager lights up and vibrates calling them to the children's building to pick up their rowdy kid(s). Children's church is nothing more than a pacifier that keeps undisciplined children corralled until big church lets out.

Here's the powerful thing about having children sit and worship with their parents in the main gathering instead of shipping them off to children's church. Masks are torn off. If a parent is having a hard time with one or more children, then the family's daily life is exposed. What's so great about that, you ask? It is great because now the church family can be a family by seeing a need and assisting. Now the church can see that the parents have been listening to Dr. Spock instead of Dr. Jesus in the training and disciplining of their children. The parents now have an opportunity to experience the sufficiency of Scripture in the area of child rearing. They get to be introduced to the politically incorrect verses such as Proverbs 23:14, "If you strike him with the rod, you will save his soul from Sheol." Or Proverbs 22:15, "Folly is bound up in the heart of a child, but the rod of discipline drives it far from him." The church now actually becomes relevant in the people's lives when it deals with real-life, everyday issues like parenting.

Households have been radically transformed by beginning to raise their kids biblically (please know that proper discipline is only one aspect of raising kids biblically and also please know that proper discipline is much more than spanking). The children in our church have grown to be more pleasant and respectful and are actually a delight to be around. I can honestly say about some of them that that was not the case prior to the change in direction of our church.

I will never forget when one of our dear saintly ladies of the church gave a testimony. To be honest with you, I was a little nervous, because I knew her testimony was about the church's directional change. She has been a member since the early sixties, so the people were waiting to hear this one! She stood up and said that she has been moved and blessed by God by seeing the change in the children of the church since they have been attending the big church. She said the children were a joy, and it was both right and great to have them as a part of the church. Tears filled my eyes not because the leadership was off the hook, but because younger parents and children alike heard this and were strengthened. This would never have happened in the secular segregation of the typical church structure. The lights have been turned on!

The Lights Have Been Turned On in Parents

I have already mentioned how parents have actually become more free not by sending their kids off but by having their kids with them in church. The freedom comes when they accept the responsibility of being a parent and raising their kids biblically. Many families have grown and flourished through this transition. I would be remiss not to say that early on some did not like having their kids with them and were not willing to walk into the light-filled room of biblical parental responsibility. They simply left and found a church down the road that would meet the perceived needs of their children. Some may say that is a harsh judgment for me to pass on someone else. Friend, look around and see that in the culture at large and even in the church, parents are oppressed by their children. Children are despised and looked at as burdens. I would bet you that those who have a problem with having their children with them in church probably have 1.6 kids in their home and are adamantly opposed to having more children than they have. What they have is all that their pocketbooks and nerves can handle. It is easy to stereotype something that is statistically accurate.

But let me just tell you something. For the parents that have had the lights turned on by God and His Word through this transition, a whole new world has opened up. Walks with the Lord have been strengthened and taken to new heights. People have been blessed beyond measure and have even pursued enlarging their families. Fathers have been empowered to lead. Purpose in marriages has been restored. A fervor for missions and evangelism burns in the hearts of the people. The lights are turning on one at a time.

Some may mistake the sanctification of the church body that we are experiencing at Ridgewood for arrogance and piety. Anyone who hangs around us a little while sees that is the farthest thing from the truth. We are truly humbled and overwhelmed. We don't have it all figured out and would never presume to say we did. Some might say, "How can you, Dustin, make a statement like you did at the beginning of the chapter saying that you all have had the lights turned on through age integration and that you all would never go back!? That is arrogant. Is it not?"

What I have written, I have written. If anyone is offended, I simply pray you can hear my heart as well as the hearts of others across our land who have heard the warning of the foghorn and have chosen to travel in a different direction from the majority. As I also stated earlier, it is not that we can't go back. It is that we won't. I for one refuse.

I close this section of the book by giving you one more incident that explains why I can't go back. And I hope you can hear the true humility of my spirit. I mentioned the blessings I receive upon having my two older girls ask what book we are going to be in at church. Well, let me tell you about a recent blessing that involved my youngest daughter. Recently, my wife and I adopted our third little girl. She was born in February of 2008 on a Wednesday; we found out about her on Thursday; and she came home with us from the hospital on Friday. She is beautiful, and she is our joy. Our new daughter has Trisomy 21 which is Down syndrome. We found out later that she has a congenital heart defect that will require open-heart surgery just a few weeks from my typing these words. Several weeks ago I was holding her during our Sunday morning church gathering while we were singing as a congregation. We were singing the song "He Knows My Name" when the Spirit of God overwhelmed me and I wept and rejoiced. My little girl, whom many in the world deem weak and worthless, *has a Maker who formed her **heart**, and even before time began her life was in His hands. He knows her name!* In that worshipful moment with my family around me, I again "discerned what is the will of God, what is good and acceptable and perfect" (Romans 12:2). That memorable and empowering moment with my God would not and could not have ever happened if my baby girl was in a nursery while my other two girls were off at children's church. I will not go back. The ship stays the course.

Part 2

The Directions for the Journey

Chapter 5

When Men Knew No Better
The Means of Church Growth

Acts 2:37–47

Opponents of the movement toward age integration in the church usually point their criticisms toward the age-integrated church's rejection of modern-day youth and children's ministries. I am sure the first part of this book, in which children's church is singled out, only adds fuel to the fire for the opponents of age integration. The irony of it all for integrated churches is that the youth and children are just a small part of who they are as a church, and yet their opponents are the ones who want to make the conversation only about youth and children. Since children and youth ministry are big business, it is only natural for integrated opponents to make children and youth their battle cry against the age-integrated movement. Without the numbers of children and youth in the modern-day church market, there would be no bread to butter. Children and youth are the bread. In my denomination alone, baptisms of children and youth from the ages of 0 to 17 comprise the majority of annual baptisms.[1] It is not hard to see why people are so sensitive concerning any change that might just rock the boat concerning modern-day children's and youth programs.

Age-integrated churches are not just concerned about one defined segregated group; rather, they are concerned for the well-being of the whole body. Integrated churches simply have the desire to be healthy churches. They have a sincere burden to do church God's way according to His Word. They do not claim to be perfect. They just claim that the head of the church, Jesus Christ, is perfect. They have a sincere belief that His ways are the best. It is to Christ that all churches must submit.

When the Lord started to challenge us at Ridgewood, our "churched" instinct was to find the latest book or program that could help us out. As we looked, there seemed to be nothing that was focused on what was transpiring in our hearts. All we could do was ask the Lord for wisdom. He turned us to what He has already revealed in His Book. Imagine that! We turned to the Bible. What we found transformed us and has brought us on an exciting journey. This transformation is an ongoing process. In our pursuit to truly be people of the Book and to be as biblical as possible, the Pandora's box was opened. Just when the Lord saw us through one area of change, He immediately brought another area that needed change to our attention. Age integration is nothing more than seeing that the body is whole, complete, and healthy not severed, lacking, and sick.

The Lord brought us to the early church in the book of Acts, particularly Acts 2:37–47. This was the time in the history of the church when men knew no better. In fact, they didn't know much about church at all. They just knew that Jesus lived, died, and rose again and that now, empowered by the Holy Spirit, they could not help but testify about Him and His works. The working of the early church that Luke recorded is about as pure as the church has ever been in its history. Church historian Philip Schaff wrote this about the early church in talking about its purity:

> We can form no clear conception of this bridal season of the Christian church when no dust of earth soiled her shining garments, when she was wholly absorbed in the contemplation and love of her divine Lord, when he smiled down upon her from his throne in heaven, and added daily to the number of the saved.[2]

For the next three chapters we will turn our attention to Acts 2 and look at three facets of growing church God's way. We will look at the means, the message, and the method of church growth from Acts 2:37–47 that reads as follows:

> Now when they heard this they were cut to the heart, and said to Peter and the rest of the apostles, "Brothers, what shall we do?" And Peter said to them, "Repent and be baptized every one of you in the name of Jesus Christ for the forgiveness of your sins, and you will receive the gift of the Holy Spirit. For the promise is for you and for your children and for all who are far off, everyone whom the Lord our God calls to himself." And with many other words he bore witness and continued to exhort them, saying, "Save yourselves from this crooked generation." So those who received his word were baptized, and there were added that day about three thousand souls. And they devoted themselves to the apostles' teaching and the fellowship, to the breaking of bread and prayers. And awe came upon every soul, and many wonders and signs were being done through the apostles. And all who believed were together and had all things in common. And they were selling their possessions and belongings and distributing the

proceeds to all, as any had need. And day by day, attending the temple together and breaking bread in their homes, they received their food with glad and generous hearts, praising God and having favor with all the people. And the Lord added to their number day by day those who were being saved.

The Means of Biblical Church Growth

The first aspect of church growth we'll look at is the means of church growth. Typically the *means* of anything is simply the tool that is used to achieve a desired result. Often the means can also be called the method or program. In this particular instance when I talk about the means of church growth, I am not referring to the method (that will be discussed two chapters later); rather, I am referring to the One who is the means to the method. The means of church growth is the *who* and not the *how or what.* Often strategies and programs are implemented without any thought of the origin or means of the strategy or program itself. We'll briefly look at three aspects from Acts 2:37–47 of the means of pure biblical church growth. They will be looked at as challenges for all who are in Christendom to embrace.

Surrender to God's Will, Not to Man's Futile Thinking

There was one thing that the leaders of the early church knew that needs to be recaptured in churches across our land. They knew that God was in control and man was not. The early church understood that God in His sovereignty would accomplish His redemptive plan in spite of man. They understood that no man who dwells in the natural, created world can thwart the purposes of the supernatural God who is the Creator of all that is seen and unseen. For example, in Acts 4:24–30 after John and Peter were released from the authorities, the members of the early church lifted their voices together and cried out:

> Sovereign Lord, who made the heaven and the earth and the sea and everything in them, who through the mouth of our father David, your servant, said by the Holy Spirit, "Why did the Gentiles rage, and the peoples plot in vain? The kings of the earth set themselves, and the rulers gathered together, against the Lord and against his Anointed" for truly in this city there were gathered together against your holy servant Jesus, whom you anointed, both Herod and Pontius Pilate, along with the Gentiles and the peoples of Israel, to do whatever your hand and your plan had predestined to take place. And now, Lord, look upon their threats and grant to your servants to continue to speak your word with all boldness, while you stretch out your hand to heal, and signs and wonders are performed through the name of your holy servant Jesus.

The members of the early church completely surrendered themselves to the fact that no one was able to stop God's plan of redemption, and they understood that they needed Him to grant them continuance of their ministry to see His plan fulfilled.

Immediately following Peter's first sermon in Acts 2, Luke narrates for us that God was the means of the early growth of the church. In verses 39 and 47 he states, "For the promise is for you and for your children and for all who are far off, everyone whom the Lord our God calls to himself . . . And the Lord added to their number day by day those who were being saved."

The Lord Himself was the means to church growth that produced the end result that He had planned. Does this exclude man from the equation of church growth? Not at all! I am just trying to show that God was the ultimate means or source by which growth came. The church did in fact grow in conjunction with either the obedience or disobedience of individuals in that first-century setting of the early church. From the Scripture passages quoted from Acts, we observe that the individual choices made by Herod, Pontius Pilate, the Gentiles, and the Jews were the earthly cause of the death of the Anointed One, while the individual choices of Peter, John, and the other followers of Christ were the earthly cause of seeing thousands saved unto God. Every individual was responsible before a holy God for his or her actions. Peter told the crowd they were responsible for killing Jesus when he said, "Let all the house of Israel therefore know for certain that God has made him both Lord and Christ, this Jesus whom you crucified" (Acts 2:36).

Again, let me stress my point that it is God who is the means behind biblical growth. Many in our day would argue that the means to church growth is our God-given charisma, ingenuity, and creativity that is put forth in programs; hence, if a church isn't growing by the ABC's (Attendance, Buildings, and Cash), then the problem must be with the pastor or other leaders and their lack of charisma, ingenuity, and creativity or their choice of programming. I would argue that it is man's reliance upon his own futile thinking that is behind the grim state of Christianity in our day. (Please refer back to chapters 1 and 2.) Many of today's church leaders sit around the white marker board to discuss new ways they can attract people. When the people do arrive, every little nuance of comfort and appeal is in place and in order to produce a desired response from all who have entered. Calendars are marked years in advance with revival services and baptismal services as if God is at the mercy of moving only when people say when. Leaders opt to forgo Bible conferences for creative conferences put on by those who have figured out how to attract the most people on a given weekend.

How can churches in our day draw such large crowds while the numbers of true Christians are becoming smaller and orthodox Christianity is on the verge of extinction in the West? We must remember the old adage, "All that glitters is not gold." Proverbs 14:12 says, "There is a way that seems right to a man, but its end is the way to death." When it comes to the decline of Christianity in our day, even with all the new, innovative church-growth strategies over the last half century or so, I find a striking similarity when looking at the decline of the Roman Empire. In his classic book *How Shall We Then Live?*, Francis Schaeffer tracks the rise and decline of Western thought and culture in our society from the early days of Rome to the current day. Schaeffer lists the five attributes that marked the end of Rome as described in Edward Gibbon's *Decline and Fall of the Roman Empire* that was written in the late 1700s. Schaeffer uses these attributes to draw a comparison with the current state of U.S. society. Although Schaeffer's indictment was on the nation as a whole, the list hit me straight between the eyes as a proper indictment and description of the church and the current state of Christianity. I simply want to list these five attributes to allow you to make your own conclusions and comparisons.

1. A mounting love of show and luxury
2. A widening gap between the very rich and the very poor
3. An obsession with sex
4. Freakishness in the arts, masquerading as originality, and enthusiasm pretending to be creativity
5. An increased desire to live off the state.[3]

These five attributes that ushered in the end of the Roman Empire are currently threatening the future of the United States of America and are having a damning effect inside the modern-day church. God is looking for a people who will wholeheartedly surrender to His will and not to man's futile thinking.

Trust in God's Word, Not in Man's Foolish Tongue

Not only do we see the early church surrendering to God's will, we also see them trusting in God's Word. Guys like Peter were rough, rugged fishermen. They were not concerned with looking hip, wearing power colors, or having bleached teeth. The men in the early church didn't rehearse in front of the mirror and certainly didn't have researchers and writers on staff. They didn't have the technological advances of the twenty-first century to enhance or streamline their messages. They weren't even concerned if their message offended anyone or not. They were "average men who were selected from the unworthy and the unqualified."[4] They were not trained in debate and were not educated like the elite. Yet, their powerful message mixed with their uncomely appearance and stature led to the baffling of the religious leaders "when they saw the boldness of Peter and John, and perceived that they were uneducated, common men" (Acts 4:13). Peter and John trusted in the proclamation of the Word of God and did not rely upon the craftiness of a silver tongue.

There are two verses we often hear in church life that are used for two different situations. The first verse says, "Not many of you should become teachers, my brothers, for you know that we who teach will be judged with greater strictness" (James 3:1). This verse is usually brought up as a heed or caution when someone is contemplating surrendering to the full-time ministry or is accepting an invitation to teach for the first time in a Sunday-school setting or the like. It is also used by teachers to describe the weight they carry when they are to teach from God's Word. The second verse I want to bring up is the famous passage that says, "No human being can tame the tongue" (James 3:8). This particular verse and passage is used usually in speaking out against cursing or maligning other people. The way these two verses have been used in church life in our day might make you conclude that these two verses are in no way connected. They are looked upon as stand-alone verses that are used for stand-alone situations. It would probably surprise many that these verses are directly connected in context in James chapter 3. When they are put together in the entire passage, a whole new meaning opens up. Read the passage below from James 3:1–10 and see what I mean.

> Not many of you should become teachers, my brothers, for you know that we who teach will be judged with greater strictness. For we all stumble in many ways. And if anyone does not stumble in what he says, he is a perfect man, able also to bridle his whole body. If we put bits into the mouths of horses so that they obey us, we guide their whole bodies as well. Look at the ships also: though they are so large and are driven by strong winds, they are guided by a very small rudder wherever the will of the pilot directs. So also the tongue is a small member, yet it boasts of great things. How great a forest is set ablaze by such a small fire! And the tongue is a fire, a world of unrighteousness. The tongue is set among our members, staining the whole body, setting on fire the entire course of life, and set on fire by hell. For every kind of beast and bird, of reptile and sea creature, can be tamed and has been tamed by mankind, but no human being can tame the tongue. It is a rest-

less evil, full of deadly poison. With it we bless our Lord and Father, and with it we curse people who are made in the likeness of God. From the same mouth come blessing and cursing. My brothers, these things ought not to be so.

Wow! When the two often-quoted passages are read in context, they take on a whole new meaning. Teachers indeed are to take heed specifically when it comes to what their futile tongues teach for the tongue is powerful, uncontrollable and is the cause of much evil.

Modern-day teachers must not assume that the slyness of their tongues and craftiness of their presentations are the means to their success. The message to be preached is not to be compromised, tainted, or outright neglected. People are not to be manipulated and steered emotionally by the whip of the tongue. Buzz words like *repentance*, *sin*, and *wrath* are not to be redefined or ignored. God's Word is alive and powerful and is not in need of any man-made extras or calculations to make it somehow more relevant, palatable, and effective.

My wife and I came across a late-night Christian talk show this past year that had an up-and-coming pastor and his wife on the show as guests. The talk-show hosts were enamored with the creativity of the pastor's messages and how he used elaborate stage props to get his message across. Sermon highlights showed the on-stage use of a human canon, cars, motorcycles, ping pong tables, etc. Then the comment was made by the guests that if Jesus were alive today, they believe this is how He would communicate His message with people, for after all, Jesus did speak in parables. All that my wife could say to me after that statement was, "Dustin, why do you even put yourself through this?" to which all I could reply was, "May God help us 'cause we're in trouble."

So what did I do to bring peace to my agitated spirit? I went on YouTube to search for more highlights from this pastor (not a good idea for me because I can't ever recover the lost hours of sleep from that night). I came across a video produced to show how this pastor and his team come up with his messages. I'm sure he is a great guy, and he looks like he would be fun to hang out with. It would be totally safe, however, to say that he and I have different interpretations of what the early church leaders meant in Acts 6:4 when they said, "We will devote ourselves to prayer and to the ministry of the word." You can visit www.youtube.com/watch?v=nQ5GDB4P1XM to see this popular and widely accepted interpretation of Acts 6:4.

Let's look at the early church and how they got their message across. How did they do it? How were they able to see thousands saved in one day? Well, as already stated in the first point, they surrendered to God's will. Second, to restate the point of this section, they trusted in the power of God's Word. They did not back away from preaching truth. They preached the whole counsel of God's Word. In Peter's Acts 2 sermon, he quoted the prophet Joel once and David twice. He preached Jesus crucified, risen, and exalted. He called men lawless and implied they were murderers. And what was the response of the hearers of the sermon? Verse 37 says, "Now when they heard this they were cut to the heart, and said to Peter and the rest of the apostles, 'Brothers, what shall we do?'" And how did Peter respond to them in verse 38? "Peter said to them, 'Repent and be baptized every one of you in the name of Jesus Christ for the forgiveness of your sins, and you will receive the gift of the Holy Spirit.'"

I guess can we can say today that Peter and the early church just didn't know any better when they called people to repent and talked about sin and stuff. It sounds kind of boring and plain and abrasive to me.

The early church was committed to God's Word. It says in Acts 2:42 that "they devoted themselves to the apostles' teaching." Paul, in Ephesians 2:19b–22, says that believers "are fellow citizens with the saints and members of the household of God, built on the foundation of the apostles and prophets, Christ Jesus himself being the cornerstone, in whom the whole structure, being joined together, grows into a holy temple in the Lord. In him you also are being built together into a dwelling place for God by the Spirit."

God's Word is the foundation of true church growth. We are to reject the futile messages of our times to which so many are flocking. We are to accept the directive that Paul gives Timothy in 2 Timothy 4:1–5.

> I charge you in the presence of God and of Christ Jesus, who is to judge the living and the dead, and by his appearing and his kingdom: preach the word; be ready in season and out of season; reprove, rebuke, and exhort, with complete patience and teaching. For the time is coming when people will not endure sound teaching, but having itching ears they will accumulate for themselves teachers to suit their own passions, and will turn away from listening to the truth and wander off into myths. As for you, always be sober-minded, endure suffering, do the work of an evangelist, fulfill your ministry.

Implement God's Way, Not Man's Failed Tactics

I'm sure you have gathered, in exploring age integration in the church thus far, that those of us in the church-integration movement believe that man's pragmatic tactics in church life have failed. I'll refrain at this time from belaboring the failures of modern church at this juncture since you probably think I have done enough of that already. (Please note that I said I'll refrain at this time, but I cannot make any promises about future rantings.)

Let's turn to the positive side of this third point of understanding that God is the means behind biblical church growth. It is only logical to declare that God has ways for His church to operate that fall in line with His will and His Word. We will quickly look at the implementation of God's way in regard to the functioning of the local church. Again we turn to the church in Acts 2 in order to observe their practices.

There were several practices in which the early church participated in Acts 2 such as devoting themselves to the apostles' teaching, fellowship, breaking of bread, prayers, giving, praising God, going from house to house, and eating meals together. When I refer to implementing God's ways, I am referring to how all of these practices mentioned were implemented and practiced. They were all practiced together. God's way for His church to operate and grow is by the togetherness of His people when they practice corporately their faith. Verse 42 says, "They were . . ." Other plural descriptions in verses 42–47 are "every soul," "all," "were together," "all things in common," "they were," "to all," "together," "their homes," "they received," "their food," "hearts," "all the people," and "the Lord added to their number." The early church did things together! They were not separated or segregated. They were in fact age integrated. They were a multigenerational community of believers.

Here is what jumped out at us at Ridgewood as the Lord was integrating every facet of the church: it was the early church's togetherness that was the platform for the gospel. Look in verse 47. It says that they were "praising God and *having favor with all the people. And the Lord added to their number* day by day those who were being saved" (italics added). If we jump ahead to Acts 4:32–33, we again see the power of God being manifested to the world through the togetherness of His people.

Now the full number of those who believed were of one heart and soul, and no one said that any of the things that belonged to him was his own, but they had everything in common. And with great power the apostles were giving their testimony to the resurrection of the Lord Jesus, and great grace was upon them all.

The fact that the Lord used the togetherness of His people to promote the gospel to a lost and dying world should come as no surprise to Christians. Jesus Himself said that the one distinguishing quality or characteristic that will not only make His people different from the world but will also make the world take notice of Him and His people is love (demonstrated by togetherness, unity, and fellowship). Jesus said in John 13:34–35, "A new commandment I give to you, that you love one another: just as I have loved you, you also are to love one another. By this all people will know that you are my disciples, if you have love for one another." When Jesus was praying His high priestly prayer in John 17, He said in verses 20–23:

> I do not ask for these only, but also for those who will believe in me through their word, that they may all be one, just as you, Father, are in me, and I in you, that they also may be in us, so that the world may believe that you have sent me. The glory you have given me I have given to them, that they may be one even as we are one, I in them and you in me, that they may become perfectly one, so that the world may know that you sent me and loved them even as you loved me.

Jesus could not have been clearer that He wants to bring God's glory to the entire world through the testimony of the togetherness of His children: His church. It is also important to note that the church is called "the body" in the New Testament. God explicitly shows us how important it is for the body to operate as a unit rather than separately. The passage in 1 Corinthians 12:12–27 supports this:

> Just as the body is one and has many members, and all the members of the body, though many, are one body, so it is with Christ . . . For the body does not consist of one member but of many. If the foot should say, "Because I am not a hand, I do not belong to the body," that would not make it any less a part of the body. And if the ear should say, "Because I am not an eye, I do not belong to the body," that would not make it any less a part of the body. If the body were an eye, where would be the sense of hearing? If the whole body were an ear, where would be the sense of smell? But as it is, God arranged the members in the body, each one of them as he chose. If all were a single member, where would the body be? As it is, there are many parts, yet one body. The eye cannot say to the hand, "I have no need of you," nor again the head to the feet, "I have no need of you." On the contrary, the parts of the body that seem to be weaker are indispensable, and on those parts of the body that we think less honorable we bestow the greater honor, and our unpresentable parts are treated with greater modesty, which our more presentable parts do not require. But God has so composed the body, giving greater honor to the part that lacked it, that there may be no division in the body, but that the members may have the same care for one another. If one member suffers, all suffer together; if one member is honored, all rejoice together. Now you are the body of Christ and individually members of it.

I do hope you did not skip over that passage. If you did, go back and read it. While reading it, ask yourself this question: Which church, an age-segregated one or an age-integrated one, best represents God's desire for His church to function together as a body? I am sure you know my answer to that question.

The beauty of the age-integrated church is that everyone is important, no matter his or her age. Young and old relate with one another for the proper functioning of the body. The age-integrated church greatly reduces bitter remarks from the adults about "ungrateful kids" and significantly diminishes disrespectful remarks from the kids about the "boring old people."

Gone are the days at an age-integrated church where a family pulls up in a church parking lot and waves good-bye to each other only to tell each other hello when they return to their car to leave the church premises. Age-integrated churches have a sincere desire to implement God's means of togetherness to see that their faith is shared with a lost and dying world, but also that their children and their children's children will live the faith in the context of a biblical community while being a witness to their own respective generation and the generations to come.

My hope for my children is that when they are pulled out of my quiver and shot off into this dark world that wherever they land they will have a desire to join a local community of like-minded believers: a church. What will instill this desire to join a body of believers when they are older? The desire will be born of the multigenerational relationships that they, their parents, and so many others relied on for strength, encouragement, and support. The desire will be based upon the fact that they have always been together with the whole church and they witness constantly the supernatural power of the gospel that is revealed through the unity and togetherness of the whole church.

Tears come to my eyes as I am writing this and thinking of all the rich relationships that span generations that my children are experiencing right now. The sight of my two oldest daughters hugging an 85-year-old single woman after we took her out for her birthday recently will forever be etched in my mind, and I hope it will be in my girls' minds as well. Seeing the excitement of my children running to "Mema" and "Pepa" to give them a hug every time they see them when we gather as a church is definitely a moment that money cannot buy. You see, "Mema" and "Pepa" are not the grandparents of my children. They are an elderly couple who are the lone remaining founding members of Ridgewood Baptist Mission back in 1958. It is God's way for His people to be together and not separated. The fruit of togetherness is lasting. God's ways are eternal while man's tactics will always fail. All the saints will be integrated together on that glorious day when we sing in unison the song of the redeemed to our God who is the means behind His own success and glory.

Chapter 6

E. F. . . . E. F. . . . E. F. Hutton
The Message of Church Growth

Acts 2:37–47

Who can ever forget the early 1980s commercial that made the stock brokerage company, E. F. Hutton, a household name? In the commercial the teacher asked her class who would like to recite the ABC's. A cute little girl with braided pigtails stood up gladly and started to say the ABC's. "A B C D E F . . . E F . . . E. F. Hutton!" she proudly proclaimed. As soon as she says "E. F. Hutton," all of her classmates leave their desks and circle around her with tuned-in ears expecting to hear something grand. The voice-over comes on at this moment and says the company's tagline, "When E. F. Hutton talks, people listen." The irony today is that E. F. Hutton is not even in existence to speak anything at all to anybody. After hard times and a big kiting scandal, the great company lost its name in a merger in 1988. This goes to show that cute, man-made slogans and marketing schemes are passing and fading and offer no guarantees. Any message that the world puts forth in any arena or for any product will simply run its course.

The early church knew that God had given them a message that was eternal and would transcend all times and cultures. When we turn back to Scripture as our guide for church growth, we find that God has given His people the message for true church growth. God has chosen His revealed Word to be the message that is to be proclaimed. Church slogans and seeker-sensitive marketing ideas are ever changing according to the times and demographical statistics of the day, but God's Word is settled in heaven for all of eternity and will not fade off into the sunset of yesteryear. At the heart of the age-integrated-church movement is the understanding and appreciation of the Word of God and its relevancy to all people groups of all times. This in no way implies that age-integrated churches don't recognize the differences of certain cultures or don't seek to know who the people are in the community they are trying to reach. This also doesn't mean that age-integrated churches don't have church mottos, vision statements, professional websites, and/or promotional materials to explain who they are as a church. They simply allow God's Word to define who they are instead of the current church trends of the day.

We would rather give God's Word to households to see Him work in their lives instead of giving them surveys to see how their darkened hearts can enlighten us on how we are to work in our church life.

In this chapter I want to expand on trusting God's Word. I hope to define exactly what the message that is to be proclaimed in church life is, as well as look to Acts 2 to see how God uses this message to change lives and further His purposes here on earth.

The Necessity of Preaching the Whole Counsel of God's Word

The message that the church is to declare to see true church growth is purely God's Word. The Bible, from Genesis to Revelation, is to be proclaimed without compromise. The submission of a people to the whole counsel of God's Word is at the heart of the age-integrated movement. As Paul states in the latter part of Ephesians 2, the foundation of the church is the teachings of the prophets and apostles with Christ being the cornerstone.

This submission to the whole counsel of God's Word means that nothing in the Bible is off-limits, not even the Old Testament. As mentioned in chapter 5, the early church leaned heavily upon God's revealed Word at the time (the Old Testament). Again, that can be seen in Peter's Acts 2 sermon when he quotes both Joel and David. If we continue in the book of Acts, we observe Stephen in chapter 7 using the history of the Jews as recorded in the Old Testament to set the stage for the good news of the gospel he preached to his persecutors, while we see Phillip in Acts 8 using Isaiah 53:7–8 as the basis for his sharing the gospel with the Ethiopian eunuch. Jesus also referred to the Old Testament in talking about Himself in Luke 4 and 24. The first being His use of Isaiah 61:1–2 while the latter was the time He told His walking buddies on the journey to Emmaus about His resurrection as foretold in all the Scriptures starting with Moses and then the prophets.[1]

The message is contained in all of the Bible not just parts of it. The best way, in my belief, to preach the whole counsel of God's Word is through expository preaching. In fact, references to Stephen, Phillip, and Jesus above all were instances where Scripture was expounded.[2] Mark Dever, in his book *Nine Marks of a Healthy Church*, lists expositional preaching as Mark 1. Dever defines expositional preaching by stating:

Expositional preaching is not simply producing a verbal commentary on some passage of Scripture. Rather, expositional preaching is that preaching which takes for the point of a sermon the point of a particular passage of Scripture. That's it. The preacher opens the Word and unfolds it for the people of God.[3]

In relation to the importance of the church preaching the whole counsel of God's Word expositionally, Dever continues:

Preaching should always (or almost always) be expositional because the Word of God should be at its center, directing it. In fact, churches should have the Word at their center, directing them. God has chosen to use His Word to bring life. That's the pattern we see in Scripture and in history. His Word is His own chosen instrument for bringing life.[4]

The Word of God must be preached in context with no part or passage ever remaining untouchable or irrelevant for His people. The author of Hebrews states in Hebrews 4:12 that "the word of God is living and active, sharper than any two-edged sword, piercing to the division of soul and of spirit, of joints and of marrow, and discerning the thoughts and intentions of the heart." God's Word is the message of church growth, and I want to quickly point out five ways that God's Word was used by God to grow His church in Acts 2.

The Word of God Takes Priority over the Church and Its Practices

Notice that the very first practice or activity in Acts 2:42–47 is that "they devoted themselves to the apostles' teaching." It can be logically deduced that all of the following practices of the early church in that context in no way contradicted the teaching that they were devoted to. Ephesians 2:19–20 states that the apostles and prophets are the foundation on which the household of God is built. The practices of the church must rest firmly on the solid foundation of the Bible. To put it plainly, the Word of God comes before the church and its practices. The church does not define the Word of God. It is the Word of God that defines the church.

One of the main problems and perplexities that caused me to leave my childhood faith of Roman Catholicism was the Vatican's belief that both Scripture and church tradition were to be held in equal veneration and that both were to be submitted to equally. The Roman Catholic Church holds that both the Word of God and the Church of Rome are infallible, meaning they cannot err. There were, and still are, two main problems with this for me. First, the Pope (when sitting in Peter's chair which is termed *ex cathedra*) allegedly infallibly interprets the Word of God that is already declared infallible. Thus the Church, led by fallible man, actually negates its own stance that the Word of God is infallible by subjecting God's Word to the supposedly infallible interpretation of the Church. The Church at this point is the foundation for the Bible and not vice versa. The Church at this point takes precedence over the Word of God. Second, my problem is that there are a myriad of Roman Catholic supposedly infallible traditions and practices that directly contradict what is revealed in the infallible Word of God. Logic dictates that if Church teaching *A* and Bible text *B* are in direct contradiction with each other, then either *A* is right and *B* is wrong, or *B* is right and *A* is wrong, or both *A* and *B* are wrong. They both cannot be exclusively right, however. Both *A* and *B* cannot diametrically oppose each other and both be right and both maintain their infallibility.

Most of you reading this are probably Protestants or evangelicals, and you are saying wholeheartedly, "Amen to that brother!" But do you know what I have observed since I have chosen to be a Baptist? Baptists are often guilty of the same Roman Catholic heresy just mentioned with the difference being that Baptists don't have it written down on paper anywhere. Although Baptists say they submit to God's Word alone and not to a man-made institution, just go ahead and try to usher in change in a Baptist church that challenges from a biblical standpoint a tradition or practice of that particular church. Have you ever heard some good ol' boy Baptist beat his chest while exclaiming, "I don't care what the Bible says, this is the way we've always done it, and this is the way we're gonna keep a doin' it!" If you ever hear anyone say this or something of the sort, go ahead and pull up a chair for them and print up a paper that says "*ex cathedra*" and tape it to the chair. Many times Baptists become guilty of allowing their church traditions or practices to define God and His Word. At that moment the church takes priority over the Word. This is wrong and heretical.

A big part of the age-integrated-church movement is that people are willing to have their church upbringings and presuppositions challenged and changed by the Word of God, because it is the Word of God that takes priority over the church.

The Word of God Penetrates the Culture at Large

As a pastor, I cannot tell you the amount of junk mail I receive daily. All kinds of solicitations to try this or do this or attend this mostly end up in file thirteen for me. There was one flyer/postcard that caught my attention; I knew it would make a good illustration, so I refrained from throwing it away. On the front was a cartoon picture of a preacher with an armadillo strapped on his head. The talking balloon above his head read, "I don't know why this isn't working." The other side of the card was an advertisement for some kind of Power Team wannabes and it boasted in its guarantee to attract large crowds and produce many "decisions" for Christ. I wasn't quite sure if it amused me or made me nauseous. The modern-day church will do just about anything to dupe, I mean attract, a large crowd with a huge production only to trickily offer up a five-minute canned gospel invitation at the end. The pragmatic reasoning behind this is, "We need to do whatever it takes to reach the culture of our day. If entertainment is what they like, then entertainment is what we'll give them!"

The early church didn't jump through hoops to disguise the gospel or hide their desire of wanting to see souls saved. They preached the Word. They understood that the truths of God's Word can invade any culture at any time and anywhere. God will use His Word to accomplish His purpose to the uttermost parts of the earth. Peter's sermon in Acts 2 was a singular message that was preached to a plethora of people from a plurality of places. Acts 2:5 describes the scene by saying, "Now there were dwelling in Jerusalem Jews, devout men from every nation under heaven." Luke then goes on and lists fourteen different places where the people in the crowd were from in verses 9–10.

Peter didn't gather the troops up and give them different assignments on how to reach the particular attendees during Pentecost. Can you just hear the meeting now? Peter says, "That's a good idea John. That would sure be a loving way to appeal to the Parthians." Then Phillip speaks up and says, "Yes that will show the way for the Parthians, but the Medes and Elamites won't understand how to get to Jesus that way."

"I doubt any of this is going to work. I'll believe it when I see it!" chimes in Thomas.

This is ridiculous. Peter preached the ordained message of God that is able to save men, women, and children from every nation, every tribe, and every tongue under heaven. The Word of God penetrated the perverse pre-Christian culture of the first century, and it is the only thing that can penetrate the perverse post-Christian culture of our twenty-first century. We can conclude our message with boldness today just as Peter did two thousand years ago. "And with many other words he bore witness and continued to exhort them, saying, 'Save yourselves from this crooked generation'" (Acts 2:40).

The Word of God Pricks the Core of a Person's Being

Immediately after Peter's discourse in Acts 2, the people responded in verse 37, "Brothers, what shall we do?" The group of people who asked this sobering question no doubt includes some of the very ones who mocked the followers of Christ before Peter's sermon in Acts 2:13 claiming the followers of Christ must be drunk. Why the change? What happened? Did Peter have music playing in the background to influence their emotions? Did Peter have everyone bow their heads and close their eyes while he told them that they could be run over by a bus, I mean camel, when they left Jerusalem so they better get right with Jesus today? Did he slowly manipulate them by leading them in a prayer, then by leading them to raise their hands, then by leading them to look directly at him, then by leading them to stand (still while no one is looking around), then lead them to walk an aisle to come to the sacred front of the church building, and then ask everyone to open their eyes to see the person standing before them that they were just forbidden to look at previously when they had their eyes closed and head bowed so as not to make them uncomfortable? God forbid! Peter preached the Word of God, and God used His Word to cut to the core of the people's being and to create new life in people who were dead in sins and trespasses.

The beginning of Acts 2:37 tells us why they spoke up and asked the above question. "Now when they heard this they were cut to the heart." These people were broken by God through the proclamation of His Word. In his expositional commentary, the eighteenth-century Baptist theologian, John Gill, wrote the following to describe what being cut to the heart meant:

> The word of God entered into them, and was as a sharp sword in them, which cut and laid open their hearts, and the sin and wickedness of them; they saw themselves guilty of the crime laid to their charge, and were filled with remorse of conscience for it; they felt pain at their hearts, and much uneasiness, and were seized with horror and trembling; they were wounded in their spirits, being hewn and cut down by the prophets and apostles of the Lord, and slain by the words of his mouth; they were as dead men in their own apprehension; and indeed, a prick, a cut, or wound in the heart is mortal.[5]

The Word of God Produces True Change in a Person's Life

The crowd, no doubt convicted of their sin, did not have to wait long to hear Peter's response to their desperate question: "Brothers, what shall we do?" Peter said in Acts 2:38, "Repent and be baptized every one of you in the name of Jesus Christ for the forgiveness of your sins, and you will receive the gift of the Holy Spirit." This one verse can cause a myriad of theological discussions, and dissensions, into which we will not delve. What I want to show from this verse is twofold. First, the Word of God produces true change in a repentant sinner's life. The Holy Spirit uses the Word of God to breathe life into a dead soul. The second point will be explored in the very next subpoint in this chapter, and it will deal with baptism. By separating repentance and baptism this way, I hope to let you know that I am in no way advocating the doctrine of baptismal regeneration.

The message proclaimed by Peter was used by God to bring in new life to those who would respond to Peter's call to repent. Peter called the sinners to repent or turn from their sins and wicked ways and to turn unto Jesus Christ the only one who saves. The beauty of repentance is not only what we turn away from, but also who we turn to. New life can only be had through Jesus Christ alone, and this new life is ushered in by the Holy Spirit of God through the proclamation of His Word.

Paul writes in Romans 10:13, "Everyone who calls on the name of the Lord will be saved." Paul then poses several questions in the verses immediately following verse 13.

> How then will they call on him in whom they have not believed? And how are they to believe in him of whom they have never heard? And how are they to hear without someone preaching? And how are they to preach unless they are sent? As it is written, "How beautiful are the feet of those who preach the good news!" But they have not all obeyed the gospel. For Isaiah says, "Lord, who has believed what he has heard from us?" So faith comes from hearing, and hearing through the Word of Christ. (Romans 10:14–17)

The Word of God Promotes Public Confession Before the People

Acts 2:41 reveals to us that three thousand souls responded to Peter's call for repentance by receiving the message that he preached on that day. It also shows that they not only heeded Peter's call to repentance, but they also obeyed his call to be baptized. "So those who received his word were baptized, and there were added that day about three thousand souls." Those who were saved were immediately baptized. Their physical water baptism by immersion was their outward confession of their inward spiritual baptism in Christ. In referring to spiritual baptism, Paul writes, "Do you not know that all of us who have been baptized into Christ Jesus were baptized into his death? We were buried therefore with him by baptism into death, in order that, just as Christ was raised from the dead by the glory of the Father, we too might walk in newness of life" (Romans 6:3–4). The mere physical act of water baptism by immersion after salvation is analogous to Paul's spiritual description.

In order for the new believers in Jesus Christ to show that they now are to walk in the newness of life in Christ, they were baptized without hesitation and without counsel. John MacArthur notes in his commentary on the book of Acts that Peter "does not allow for any 'secret disciples.'" MacArthur continues talking about the public confession of the early believers by saying, "Baptism would mark a public break with Judaism and identification with Jesus Christ. Such a public act would help weed out any conversions which were not genuine . . . That was the crucial identification, and the cost was high for such a confession."[6]

It is God's way for His people to confess their new life in Him by the act of baptism. We have come a long way in the church when we circumvent God's Word by allowing other practices to replace baptism such as praying a prayer or walking an aisle as the practice for public confession. The early church only had one practice of public confession and that was baptism. In George Barna's latest book *Pagan Christianity,* he and coauthor Frank Viola point out the disparity between the early church and the modern church:

> In our day, the "sinner's prayer" has replaced the role of water baptism as the initial confession of faith. Unbelievers are told, "Say this prayer after me, accept Jesus as your personal Savior, and you will be saved." But nowhere in all the New Testament do we find any person being led to the Lord by a sinner's prayer. And there is not the faintest whisper in the Bible about a "personal" Savior. Instead, unbelievers in the first century were led to Jesus Christ by being taken to the waters of baptism. Put another way, water baptism was the sinner's prayer in century one! Baptism accompanied the acceptance of the gospel.[7]

Baptism is important and the Word of God promotes baptism as the practice for public confession of new believers. The church needs to call people to repent and believe upon the Lord Jesus and to make their new life in Christ public by being immersed in the waters of baptism. The church must rely upon God's Word as His message for church growth.

Chapter 7

My Dad Is Bigger Than Your Dad
The Method of Church Growth

Acts 2:37–47

Every church-going Baptist knows the routine. You are at Wal-Mart and run into a friend who goes to another Baptist church in town. The conversation inevitably turns to what is going on at your respective churches. The friend starts talking about all the wonderful things going on at his or her church saying things like, "We are having so many people come that we just don't know what to do with them." Or my personal favorite, "This week so and so joined and the week before that so and so joined and the week before that. . . . It is just so exciting! God is really moving!"

In an area with more than ninety Southern Baptist churches, I always want to say in a conversation like this, "Is God moving or are another group of disgruntled Baptists moving to another temporary residence?" As soon as the ramblings about their great churches are over, they usually ask, "How many are y'all running in your services?" or "How many people were saved at y'all's service this past Sunday?"

Let's be honest. These community diatribes often turn into a "my dad is bigger than your dad" argument. My church is bigger than your church. Our "this" is better than your "that." On and on the silly and misguided pettiness continues. This is what happens when the declared ABC's of church growth become the measuring stick of success.

I recall one of our young fathers being broken over several "my dad is bigger than your dad" church conversations he had in one particular week. The others, who both attended the same church, went through the routine talking about all that God was doing on Sunday mornings and that it was so exciting to watch. You may ask, "What troubled this father about these conversations?" The problem was really fourfold. First, he knew that some of the new members this church was getting were people from a church down the road. Second, he knew that at the same time that these two people thought everything was all peaches and cream at their church, turmoil and strife were also taking place. This father was in another conversation about the same time period with a friend who was involved with the innards of this particular church and was told of the exodus of many families that were leaving this church at this time (and the Baptist revolving door of exchanging members continues). Third, this father knew how these two conversationalists lived and wasn't seeing God move in the same exciting way in the lifestyles of these boasters. Fourth, the father was disheartened because he knew that true church growth isn't about the excitement and numerical growth on Sundays. He told me that in these conversations, he wished he could have just said to them point-blank, "That's great. But can I ask you some questions? Since God is moving in such a big way, how is He moving in your life? How is He moving in you to improve your marriage and better your spouse? What about your relationship with your children? Are you leading your family in worship? Are you fulfilling the Great Commission by discipling others personally?" This father simply wanted to know, "How can churches be growing in numbers, yet have people not growing in God and His Word?"

This last question is a common concern with believers who attend an age-integrated church and get pulled into a "my dad is bigger than your dad" discussion. They are not impressed with the glitz and glamour of modern church life. In fact, most, including this father mentioned, at one time were faithful servers at churches that were driven by the desire to see an increase in nickels and noses. They bought the bill of goods that says their service at or for the church would bring them closer to the Lord's heart. What they found instead was that through all their serving at church, the hearts residing in their own households were growing farther apart. They were far away from what the Lord's heartbeat wanted for their family. Their respective churches or church ministries may have been growing, but it was at the expense of their families.

I am in no way saying that growth doesn't happen with the addition of people to a church body. Acts 2 reveals that God added people to the early church in Jerusalem. What I am trying to get across is that a church can grow numerically without growing spiritually, and a church may even decrease numerically while growing spiritually. Numbers are not the litmus test for true church growth. Numbers can come along with true church growth, but they don't have to. God is more concerned with changing hearts than with counting heads.

God is all for growing His church. He just doesn't use programs as the method. Instead, He uses people. God's method of church growth is you and me. I am not talking about our particular service to help our church programs grow. I am talking about how our changed lives are going to help the people who are the church grow while at the same time seeing growth in our own lives, homes, and community. Since God's method of church growth is you, the believer, I want to use an acrostic of the word *YOU* to list three things that were present in the lives of the early believers in Acts 2 that were instrumental in seeing the church grow God's way.

Y—earning to Grow in the Grace and Knowledge of Jesus Christ Has to Be a Daily Practice

Believers in the early church held to the teachings of God's Word. What is important to observe is that they did not just give lip service to God's Word. They were deeply committed to its teaching. Acts 2:42 says, "They devoted themselves to the apostles' teaching." They were devoted to learning the apostles' teachings. It can be presumed that this devotion to learn and study occurred daily as they met in their homes. Acts 2:46 says, "Day by day, attending the temple together and breaking bread in their homes . . ." Since verse 42 doesn't tell us when the believers were devoting themselves to the teaching of the apostles and other practices, it only makes sense that if "day by day" they met either in the temple or their homes that their devotion to learn would be taking place daily. We know of their devotion in verse 42, and we know that they met daily, so they were daily devoted to God's Word.

Peter knew the importance for believers to be devoted to the Word so he wrote in 1 Peter 2:2-3, "Like newborn infants, long for the pure spiritual milk, that by it you may grow up into salvation—if indeed you have tasted that the Lord is good." Peter goes on to direct his readers in 2 Peter 3:18, "Grow in the grace and knowledge of our Lord and Savior Jesus Christ. To him be the glory both now and to the day of eternity."

Sadly, biblical illiteracy rates run rampant in churches all across America. There is a widespread lack of devotion and commitment to God's Word. This makes for a lot of

Christian babies who are too sick and malnourished to grow and mature into the men or women God wants them to be. Biblical illiteracy stunts true church growth.

The Bible seems to be low on the totem pole of priorities for churchgoers. The things of this world have captured the desires of professing believers in our day. In his book, *Revolution,* George Barna says the following concerning research results:

> Although the typical believer contends that the Bible is accurate in what it teaches, he or she spends less time reading the Bible in a year than watching television, listening to music, reading other books and publications, or conversing about personal hobbies and leisure interests."[1]

The bottom line in Christianity at large is people do not have a yearning to grow in the grace and knowledge of Christ each day by feasting on His Word. Too many things have captured their attention and devotion.

One of the very first things that fueled the turning of the ship at Ridgewood was the need to fight against the biblical illiteracy that was in our midst. The national norms of biblical illiteracy and ignorance unfortunately were the norms in our congregation (as they probably are statistically in yours). The personal illustration I will use is one that will tell you where we have come from. It is an account that early on in my pastorate I relayed to the people hoping that God would show us the error of our ways and instill in His people the yearning to know Him and His Word.

To tell you this story I have to give you a quick background on myself and the Bible. Growing up as a Roman Catholic, I did not read the Bible. I did not even have my own Bible until I was sixteen and going through my confirmation process. And even then we never opened and studied it. Thanks be unto God, I took that big paperback Bible with me when I went off to college. To make a long story short, I started reading the Bible in my dorm room at the age of nineteen, and a whole new world opened up to me. I read and studied a lot and even started teaching Bible studies at the Baptist Student Union. Let's fast-forward seven years to my licensing and ordination ceremony held at Ridgewood, specifically the preceremonial ordination council. I was to take the chair before the ordination council of men at our church to be grilled and tested in the faith.

What was said haunts and drives me to this day. This comment arose jokingly but with seriousness, "What can we ask you? You know more than all of us." Here I was in a room full of men who had been Christians for twenty, thirty, and forty years and beyond, and I knew more than they did?! I had only been reading the Bible for seven years! I do not say this to boast. Rather, I am sharing this because I was broken. *This should not be. What in the world has the church been doing all these years? Man, don't people read the Bible?* I asked myself. I had been preparing for this meeting by studying appendix 3, "Ordination Comprehensive Questions," in *Rediscovering Pastoral Ministry* by John MacArthur, and all I got was the proverbial question, "Eh, tell us 'bout your testimony." My heart cried, *God help us.* And He has for when "we are faithless, he remains faithful" (2 Timothy 2:13).

Now, it is not unusual to hear several huddles of men talking theology or talking about what their families are learning from the Word. No longer are the perceived hard subjects of the Bible off-limits on Sunday mornings. Debate is lively amongst the family of believers at Ridgewood today. How awesome it is to hear people come back to you and say, "You know, I went home and studied, and I even looked it up in the Greek." Eyes are opening and a yearning is happening in the hearts of His people here at Ridgewood. We are not the only ones with this testimony. This is a frequent testimony from age-integrated churches. There is a move of God that is happening across this land, and God is using people to usher it in. The challenge for every believer is to yearn to grow daily in the Lord Jesus Christ and His Word.

O—thers' Needs and Well-Being Have to Become a Top Priority

You have probably heard the saying, "People don't care how much you know, until they know how much you care." The believers in the early church didn't walk around saying, "We're right, you're wrong, because the Bible says so!" They were not arrogant and puffed up in their minds and intellect like the religious leaders of their day. This doesn't mean that they possessed inferior knowledge. Read the book of Acts and you'll see that as these believers in the early church devoted themselves to the Word, God used them to debate the masses, the Pharisees and Sadducees, and the Roman officials such as Felix, Festus, and Agrippa. Through all the Spirit's demonstrations of the believers' superior wisdom, the early leaders remained selfless and looked to put the needs of others first.

The early church in Jerusalem was nothing more than one big family. In Acts 2 we see that the early believers learned together, ate together, fellowshipped together, prayed together, went to the temple together, sang together, and went from house to house together. Verses 44–45 demonstrate to us that this togetherness was more than just an opportunity for them to socialize and have friends and have their needs met; rather, their gatherings together gave them opportunities to sacrifice and extend friendship and meet the needs of others. "All who believed were together and had all things in common. And they were selling their possessions and belongings and distributing the proceeds to all as any had need" (Acts 2:44–45). This benevolent lifestyle by believers can also be seen in Acts 4:32–35:

> Now the full number of those who believed were of one heart and soul, and no one said that any of the things that belonged to him was his own, but they had everything in common. And with great power the apostles were giving their testimony to the resurrection of the Lord Jesus, and great grace was upon them all. There was not a needy person among them, for as many as were owners of lands or houses sold them and brought the proceeds of what was sold and laid it at the apostles' feet, and it was distributed to each as any had need.

In this passage, I just love how verses 32 and 34–35 talk about giving and meeting others' needs, while verse 33 talks about the power of their testimony that was being proclaimed. When believers put others before themselves, Jesus Christ was made known to all. The early church lived what Paul commands in Galatians 6:2, "Bear one another's burdens, and so fulfill the law of Christ."

I mentioned earlier in this book that age integration in a church is not just about the kids; rather, it is about the whole body. I want to give an example that the Lord used in my own heart to confirm to me that this movement is not just about the kids. This past Christmas about fifty of us, young and old from Ridgewood, visited a local nursing home to sing Christmas carols up and down the halls. As I had my three-year-old at the time on my shoulders walking down the hall singing, I suddenly got all choked up. I couldn't sing. All I could do was stand there with watery eyes. The Lord spoke to me softly yet powerfully. It hit me. Our society, including the church, doesn't just look at kids and youth as nuisances and financial burdens; they also look at the elderly and indigent through the same self-centered lens.

That night in that nursing home, I was looking into the eyes of human beings who were lonely and neglected. The still, small voice of God simply said, "Dustin, where is My church?" I am not talking about the church holding services at nursing homes or even our church ministering with songs at this institution. I am talking about God's people meeting the needs of others. I am talking about Christian families taking care of their own aged family members personally. Paul said plainly in 1 Timothy 5:8, "If anyone does not provide for his relatives, and especially for members of his household, he has denied the faith and is worse than the unbeliever." Here is one of the first responses I get when advising a family to take in their elderly family member in their own home. "If I could afford it, I would." Ding, ding, ding, there it is. Jesus' words about not being able to serve both God and money ring loud and clear. This same excuse is the one Christians use to snuff out life from their own loins as well. Kids are a financial liability and so are old people who cannot take care of themselves. I have opened a huge can of chicken liver bait, and I know it stinks. I know many will not like these last couple of paragraphs. I challenge you to do something. Drive around your community and take notice of two things. First, notice how many new senior complexes are being built. And second, notice how many Christians in your community and church have large homes with empty rooms. After that, you can call me and set up an old-school debate, and we can look deeper into this matter.

My point is that we need a new generation of Christians who will make the needs of others a top priority. We need to instill this selflessness in our children. Almost weekly, I ask my daughters, "Girls, if anything ever happens to Dad and Mom, will you, your husband, and your children take care of your baby sister?" The world will encourage my daughters in the future to put their Down syndrome sibling in a special community when she is older, but our God says they would be worse than unbelievers. The night my wife and I found out about this precious little girl who was being given up by her parents because of her condition, I remember saying to my weeping wife (as I was weeping also), "If we take her into our home, you know that we will never be alone again?" That question for us was not meant to deter what God wanted to do. We already knew that she was our daughter. That question was a humble statement of reality: a reality that has been defined for us by the world and is a by-product of a materialistic, godless society that despises life and has unfortunately infected the church.

U—nity Amongst Believers Has to Be More than Words to Make an Appeal to the Hearts of People

We can talk all day about desegregating the church and having the whole church interact across generations all day long, but if the hearts of the people do not believe unity is God's goal for His church, then all age integration will be done in vain. Just because people meet together and rub shoulders doesn't mean that the spirit of unity is in their midst. The early church in Acts 2 met together as we have discussed. We can read in verse 46 that the early church actually liked to meet together and did so in a genuine spirit of unity. "They received their food with glad and generous hearts." Their glad and generous hearts were not because of their food. In context, their hearts were glad and generous because of this newfound life in Christ that they all had and were experiencing together. They were unified, and because of their unity they were "having favor with all the people" (Acts 2:47). Unity amongst God's people has to be more than just mere words. Unity has to be real and genuine, and it is the unity of His people that God will use to make the appeal of the gospel to the world.

Unity in the lives of God's people depicts to the lost world the gospel of Jesus. Paul wrote in Ephesians 2:13–16:

> But now in Christ Jesus you who once were far off have been brought near by the blood of Christ. For he himself is our peace, who has made us both one and has broken down in his flesh the dividing wall of hostility by abolishing the law of commandments expressed in ordinances, that he might create in himself one new man in place of the two, so making peace, and might reconcile us both to God in one body through the cross, thereby killing hostility.

Jesus Christ not only reconciles His children to Himself, but He also reconciles His children with each other. Because of His work on the cross, people who were estranged from each other and separated, Jews and Gentiles, have now been united to form one new body. People make up this new man, and it is their unity that proves that Jesus' atoning work was sufficient and powerful.

If we continue our reading of Ephesians 2, we find the verses we have already talked about in this book concerning Jesus Christ being the cornerstone of the household of God while the teachings of the apostles and prophets are the foundation. In verses 21–22 we have the description of what exactly makes up the household of God that is being built with such a solid foundation. "In whom the whole structure, being joined together, grows into a holy temple in the Lord. In him you also are being built together into a dwelling place for God by the Spirit."

The household of God is YOU and all other believers. Believers are to be joined together like bricks in this spiritual building. Peter says in 1 Peter 2:5 that "you yourselves like living stones are being built up as a spiritual house." Unity amongst believers in the local church is not some abstract idea; unity is a concrete reality for a true church. The way that the true unity of this spiritual house can be showcased is through the gathering of God's people.

The age-integrated church recognizes the importance of the gathering of all the people to live out this unity in a real way. The integrated church also knows that when an outsider enters into this unified body, he or she will see the power of God working in the lives of His people.

Do you know what the most frequent comment we receive at Ridgewood from first-time visitors is? It goes like this, "Wow ... You guys have a mixture of all ages worshipping together. I also can't believe all of the kids that are in here and how well they behave." Right off the bat, because the church gathers together in complete unity, the testimonies of the people give witness to the power of Jesus Christ our Lord. The church is immediately relevant to real life issues for these first-time guests. The attraction to seekers at the age-integrated church isn't wrapped up in drama, music, and entertainment; rather, the attraction is unfolded through the lives of a transparent people who are gathered together for the world to see. The age-integrated church simply understands that a church is the gathering of the called-out ones, and so when they gather they don't split up. They stay together like chicks who have been gathered by the mother hen. God has a method of church growth, and He chooses people who have a yearning for His Word, a selfless care for others, and a desire to live in the power of unity. YOU are the method to church growth.

Part 3

The Discoveries of the New World

Chapter 8

The Big *BUT* Syndrome
The Obstacle That Stands in the Way

"I don't want the church to stop doing what it is doing. What you guys are doing is right, and it needs to happen. God is no doubt behind it. I support and agree with the changes, *but* it just is not for me." This statement and several others like it still blow my mind. This has been the confusing remark of several people who are no longer passengers on our ship at Ridgewood. I share this with you because *Turning the Ship* is about our journey and how we made a 180-degree turn to go against the tide of the current church culture in our land. And I in no way want to paint this journey as one void of obstacles and struggles along the way.

We have faced obstacles. Not everyone who was on the ship when we began the journey is still on it today. The good news is that as the Lord has cut branches off of the vine, He has grafted strong fruitful branches into those barren spots on the vine. We are no doubt a stronger, healthier, and more faithful community today because of our journey to becoming a multigenerational church. We have and still will have obstacles that will surface that we must deal with biblically and prayerfully, not pragmatically.

What has made the defectors' stories so intriguing, however, are comments like I quoted in opening this chapter. These statements are what we have found to be so baffling. No one has challenged the new direction we are traveling in as a church biblically. They have not challenged it theologically. Their main challenge has been one of practicality.

Because they have never seen it done this way, they are simply more comfortable finding another ship that is doing things the way they have always seen things done. When confronted out of genuine concern for their family and children's spiritual well-being to share with us any confirmation from the Lord and His Word on their decision to leave, we get absolutely nothing. All we get is, "I know what the church is doing is right, *but* . . ."

The main obstacle that will stand in the way of any church moving toward becoming an age-integrated church is not financial. In fact, an age-integrated church is cheaper to operate which only creates a greater cash flow for true ministry. You would think that this one statement about being cheaper would ignite some to start the change immediately.

What is the obstacle then if it is not money? It is what I call the "big *BUT* syndrome." This syndrome is a spiritual disease and not a physical one. It doesn't have to do with the body, but rather the mind. The symptoms of this syndrome are easy to identify. The symptoms are always accompanied with a big *but*. "I know what the Bible says, *but* . . ." "I know what I need to do, *but* . . ." "I know what is right and wrong, *but* . . ."

The obstacle that we have faced has been professing believers who have justified their decisions not based upon the unchanging truths of God's Word; rather, their decisions have been based upon experiences, circumstances, emotions, false philosophies, personal opinions, secular education, and/or just outright rebellion.

Sadly, when a professing believer keeps negating God's will and Word with excuses that start with the word *but,* their *buts* get so big that they couldn't fit through the open door God has for them even if they wanted to. Sometimes there are so many big *buts* sitting in the pews of churches that those infected with this condition will rise up (albeit slowly) and stand in front of God's open door for the church and block the whole church from going through and following God. The big *but* syndrome puts up a good fight at first and can even be a little scary to look at; however, this syndrome tires out easily and runs out of gas in the face of a long and persistent battle with truth and the people of truth.

I said this syndrome is mental. It is nothing more than what Paul calls "strongholds" in 2 Corinthians 10:3–5.

> For though we walk in the flesh, we are not waging war according to the flesh. For the weapons of our warfare are not of the flesh but have divine power to destroy strongholds. We destroy arguments and every lofty opinion raised against the knowledge of God, and take every thought captive to obey Christ.

Paul simply defines a stronghold as arguments and lofty opinions that challenge the knowledge of God. He says that these strongholds must be destroyed.

"*But* my seminary professor says . . . *But* we live in the twenty-first century . . . *But* in light of recent technology and discoveries . . . *But* my church has always . . . *But* my momma says . . . *But* my preacher says . . . *But* when I grew up . . . *But* I turned out all right. . ." I always want to say to *buts,* "*But* who really cares? Is God impressed?"

It doesn't matter who says the *but* or even where the *but* comes from. If it is inconsistent with God, His character, and

His Word, then it is a stronghold. In an academic essay by Richard Mayhue in John MacArthur's book *Think Biblically! Rediscovering a Christian Worldview,* Mayhue writes:

> In the context of 2 Corinthians, Paul would have in view any teaching on any subject that did not correspond to his apostolic instruction that had come into the church. Whether an unbeliever or a believer was responsible, whether the idea(s) came from scholars or the uneducated, whether the teaching found wide acceptance or not, all thoughts/opinions that were not *for* the knowledge of God were to be considered against the knowledge of God. Therefore, they were to be targeted for intellectual combat and ultimate elimination." (italics original)[1]

We must take every thought captive to the obedience of Christ and His Word. We must challenge every argument that stands in the way of true believers being obedient to God. The obstacle of strongholds, Paul says, can be broken down by divine power.

I love Mayhue's conclusion regarding how we are to deal with strongholds no matter where they originate. He says that we are to target them, combat them, and eliminate them. What we have discovered in facing the obstacle of big *buts* during our journey is that they cannot hide for long and they are big and easy targets. We must be willing to fight and challenge any argument and speculation with the truths of God's Word knowing that if you are indeed on God's ship, there is no obstacle that can cause you to sink. Full steam ahead and fire away, oh children of God!

Chapter 9

The Cookie-Cutter Family
Breaking the Cycle of Dysfunction

If you were hoping the imagery of the previous chapter would come to an abrupt halt with the period on the last page, your hopes will be fulfilled after I point out one more big *but* that has tried to squash the fun out of our journey. This *but* usually covers two different people groups and comes in two different questions; however, this *but* to the age-integrated church really can be stated in one question. The two questions go like this: "*But* where do single parents fit in?" and "*But* what about the kid who doesn't have either a mom or a dad or who has parents who don't go to church?"

These two questions were actually put together into one by someone early on in our transition. The inclusive question was, "I know what the church is doing is needed for some people, *but* what about me and others who don't have a cookie-cutter family like Dustin?" The cookie-cutter family argument is on the front of everyone's minds who have a hard time trying to wrap their brains around the thought of an age-integrated church.

I really don't know where to begin in kicking this *but* into the outer realms of ignorance. Do we begin with defining a cookie-cutter family? If so, who defines it? Is it a family with a dad, mom, two kids (one being a boy and the other a girl), a dog, and a cat? If so, I'm out. For starters I have three girls. (All of whom are adopted with two coming from not so "cookied" backgrounds and the other being a special-needs child. Plus we pray every day for God to bless our family with more brothers and sisters. I wonder if having kids is like the cookie special I can get at the mall: buy twelve and get the thirteenth free?) Also, I have one dog and two cats (that is one cat over the limit of a cookie-cutter family). Shall I continue in this foolishness that this cookie-cutter argument produces?

The way I would like to briefly deal with this cookie-cutter dispute is twofold. The first will come from Scripture and talk about the one underlying similarity of all believers regardless of their situation. To add to this brief upcoming discussion, refer back to part 2 of this book to be reminded that this journey of becoming an age-integrated church is about *every person* being connected to the whole body of believers.

The second will be from a couple of stories from the travels of our ship: a ship that is made up of an assortment of cookies. Cookies who are blended, have experienced divorce, are single parents, are empty-nesters, are widows, have many children, have few children, have no children, have imperfect children, have grandchildren, have great-grandchildren, have experienced loss, have adopted, have remarried, have been faithful in marriage, are struggling in marriage, are multi-cultured, are home schooled, are private schooled, are public schooled, are in college, have different religious backgrounds, have different economic portfolios, and have different hair colors such as blond, brown, red, black, gray, white, blue, and skin. You never know what cookie you will grab when you reach in the bag of membership at our multigenerational church.

The Whole Counsel of God's Word Leaves No One Out

An underlying misconception of a family-integrated or age-integrated church is that all of the sermons and messages deal with the family. This is the farthest thing from the truth. As discussed in part 2, the whole counsel of God's Word needs to be preached, taught, and studied. When the whole counsel is preached, passages that deal with every situation in life will be discussed. No one is left out when a commitment to preaching all of Scripture is made.

For example, I preached a four-week sermon series on the family a good while back from Colossians 3:18–21. If someone had come to visit during one of those four weeks, it would be easy for them to walk away saying that all we talked about was the family. What that individual would not know if they only came during that time period was that these four messages that corresponded with only four verses were a part of a continued study on the whole book of Colossians. These messages were four out of about twenty-five or so messages out of the book of Colossians, and they were the only ones of the twenty-five that dealt specifically with the family. The only reason these four dealt with the family was that the text in Colossians 3:18–21 dealt with wives, husbands, children, and fathers respectively. God and His Word are not respecters of people and their circumstances. He speaks to all, and all are held accountable.

The Pursuit of Godliness and Righteousness Does Not Change

Because God speaks to all and all are held accountable to Him and His Word, the pursuit of godliness and righteousness for God's children is the same no matter what stage of life or circumstance a believer is in. Peter's words in 1 Peter 1:13–16 leave no professing Christian out.

Preparing your minds for action, and being soberminded, set your hope fully on the grace that will be brought to you at the revelation of Jesus Christ. As obedient children, do not be conformed to the passions of your former ignorance, but as he who called you is holy, you also be holy in all your conduct, since it is written, "You shall be holy, for I am holy."

This directive is not dependent upon what cards life has dealt you. For instance, a man who is married with children and a man who has been divorced are still expected to be sexually and morally pure. Although their situations may be different, their struggles with the flesh are the same. The qualities of being a godly man for the two remain the same through any and all situations.

Let's take a single mom who does not have a husband to lead her and her children in the faith and compare her to a mom who has a godly husband who is taking on the spiritual responsibility of leading his family. Both women are to strive to be godly women. The married woman must fulfill the biblical duties of a wife as God has designed them by honoring and respecting her husband with a chaste spirit. The single woman, although void of the husband to honor and respect, must still possess a gentle and meek spirit and model to her children the proper attitude of a godly woman.

Does the single mother have more obstacles and hardships? No doubt. I am in no way trying to say the situations are one and the same. I am trying to say that the pursuit of holiness and righteousness in the two women's lives is the same. Because the two are seeking to have the same attitude manifested in their lives, both the single mom and the married mom can strengthen each other in this pursuit. They can relate to each other in this pursuit. The single mom is accepted, embraced, and helped in a multigenerational community of believers. The single mom is not isolated to only socialize with other single moms. She is family to all in the church, not just some. The commonality between the single mom and others, particularly married women, is not based on experiences; rather, it is based on Christ and His redemptive work in everyone's lives.

The principle of these two examples can be applied to all adults, young adults, and children. Holiness and righteousness must be pursued collectively by every member of the household of faith. This pursuit is done together in the context of relationships with other believers who do indeed come from different backgrounds and do have different experiences. This is the beauty and power of believers carrying one another's burdens in order to fulfill the law of Christ. (See Galatians 6:2.) Women influence women and teach the younger ones how to become godly women. Men sharpen men and are models for the young boys in their pursuit of holiness and righteousness in becoming godly men.

The Cycle of Dysfunction Must Be Broken

The latest statistics on divorce released by the Barna Research Group reveal that there is not a statistical difference between the divorce rate of married adults who are born again and married adults who are not born again. The research shows that among married people, 33 percent have gone through at least one divorce.[1]

What alarmed me the most about this recent study was the analysis from George Barna himself regarding this research:

> There no longer seems to be much of a stigma attached to divorce; it is now seen as an unavoidable rite of passage . . . Interviews with young adults suggest that they want their initial marriage to last,

but are not particularly optimistic about that possibility. There is also evidence that many young people are moving toward embracing the idea of serial marriage, in which a person gets married two or three times, seeking a different partner for each phase of their adult life.[2]

This is an alarming assessment of the state of marriage in our culture. People are not only now comfortable with divorce, but our young people actually are planning on the possibility of divorce. This is a horrific cycle that has been created that must be broken by God's people.

Even the questions of "What about the kids that don't have parents that bring them to church?" or "What about the single mom without a husband to lead her?" are by-products of this devastating cycle of divorce that has been created both in the culture at large and the church culture as well. Divorce has become so commonplace that we in the church accept it as fact and try only to ease the symptoms of it. God is looking for a people to break completely this damning cycle.

I am sure you would not be surprised to hear me say that in becoming an age-integrated church, we are determined to break this cycle and restore godly order in our homes and in our communities for generations to come. How are we hoping to see this happen? I'll use the last two questions mentioned in the previous paragraph to show you how it is happening. Sure, these are just a couple of personal testimonies, but these testimonies have come now that we have discovered the new and beautiful land on our journey.

A testimony from a single mom echoes the sentiments expressed by others who are in similar family situations. Her words demonstrate a complete understanding that the cycle of divorce must be broken and it will not be broken by a church that keeps doing the same things over and over while producing statistical failing results. The testimony went something like this, "Where has this teaching been my whole life? If I had learned or even heard this stuff in church growing up or from my family, it would have saved me a lot of heartache. I don't want my kids to experience what I have experienced, and I don't want my grandchildren to experience what my children have and are going through. I want them to be influenced by godly families. I want them to be around godly men because all the men in their lives are not good role models. I want them to break the cycle of divorce in our family."

This single parent understood that our multigenerational approach wasn't in place to take away the fun opportunities of her children attending segregated programs and the youth ministry. It wasn't, as some have maligned, that we don't love children. We take an age-integrated approach because we do love them and do care about their future and their children's future. She wanted her kids to have godly male influence. She wanted her children to see for the first time in their lives what a godly family looks like and how they are to function.

When children or youth come into any of our gatherings, they are taken in not exclusively by a group of their peers, but they are taken in by a family with a dad, mom, and children. They have mentors and models. After all, if these kids cannot see a biblical model of family firsthand in the church, when will they ever see it? This heart to model for our young people does not come with entertainment or programs. It is happening with God's people who are getting their hands dirty to make a difference in the lives of others. We are striving to break the cycle of dysfunction in households all across our community. We are investing in the lives of our young people today to reach the masses tomorrow.

As I am writing this, one precious young girl keeps coming to my mind. She is a girl who lives with a grandmother who is doing the best she can. The grandmother's health keeps her from getting out of their tiny apartment. We have several families who make it a point to pick up this precious girl and bring her to the gathering of the church. Right now, a godly woman, also a grandmother herself, has taken the lead with this girl in having discussions dealing with salvation and baptism. This is the church at work: discipling, modeling, and mentoring.

An Encouraging Testimony from an Elderly Saint

During this journey, Pastor Kyle and I were invited to lead a break-out session at a church leadership conference. To be completely honest with you, we didn't think we would have anyone choose our class as our class was the only one dealing with the age-integrated church. There were only 120 attendees, and they had some twenty sessions to choose from. All of the other sessions dealt with segregated church ministries. To our surprise, more than twenty people came to our class. I remember waiting to see if anybody would actually come during the first time slot to hear what we had to say. One of the very first persons to enter the room was a little old lady that if I were to guess would be in her late seventies or early eighties. She sat in the far back right corner all by herself. This dear saint of God was one of the last ones to leave the room. While I was engaged in lively debate after our session ended, Kyle went over and talked to this woman. She told Kyle with tears in her eyes, "You young guys keep doing what you're doing. It is about time somebody tried to make a difference." She went on to tell about her frustration of being a part of a church that is filled with old people like her whose children, grandchildren, and great-grandchildren are not in church. Her heart was broken for generations that were lost and for an apathetic church that wants to keep doing the very same thing that has seen their children slip through the cracks. This elderly saint got it, and she was a huge cheerleader for us to stay the course because the cycle of dysfunction must be broken.

Chapter 10

Million Dollar Question
The Answer Is No

Of all of the questions that we receive (and you have probably noticed, we get a lot of questions from a lot of people about our journey), there is one question that I have actually changed my answer on during this journey. In the beginning stages of seeing our ship turned, I would have answered this question, "Yes, I believe it can." Now since we have made the journey and the ship has been fully turned, I would answer the same question with an emphatic no.

When this question is posed by someone inquiring about our being an age-integrated church, I first smile and chuckle saying, "That is the million dollar question that everyone has." Then immediately my face goes solemn, and I say sharply, "No." You should see their reactions when I hit them with an unexpected, stern no. They breathe a sigh of relief when they realize that although I am very serious with my answer in the negative, I am simply using a little dry humor to usher in the one response that they did not want to hear. I then go on and tell them why I have changed my answer from yes to no.

I just realized that I haven't even told you what the million dollar question is. The million dollar question goes something like this, "Dustin, do you feel that this age-integrated approach of ministry can coexist with the traditional segregated approach to ministry?" If you were expecting a more profound question, I do apologize. That is the question. People want to know if they can have their cake and eat it too. They want to know if it is possible to have the best of both worlds under one roof. Since the question is usually being asked by someone who only knows church life with age-segregated ministries and programs, he or she wants to know if a family-integrated group or cell can coexist alongside all the other groups. (Wouldn't this then make the age-integrated group another segregated group? Kind of defeats the purpose, doesn't it?)

As I have said, early on in our transition I thought that we could run both sets of ministry tracks parallel to each other. Boy was I wrong. To be fair, I should add to my current answer of no to the million dollar question by saying, "It may work, but only for a little while." Even with my new addendum, my answer really doesn't change. Churches can try, and we did, but eventually there will come a time when people will realize that although these two ship channels are running parallel to each other, what you have is two different ships traveling in opposite directions. You will have two different groups of people who will have two different ideas of church. I will concede that a pocket of family-integrated mind-set groups can, and probably do, exist in large megachurch settings where small communities of like-minded believers can become almost a community or church unto themselves apart from the megachurch as a whole. If those groups exist, they won't be able to see the megachurch itself change in the direction they are convicted the church needs to go; hence, my answer is still no.

Turning the Ship

One of the first things we implemented at Ridgewood was nothing more than a family-integrated Sunday-school class. (Before I go on to share our experience, you have more than likely picked up on the fact that we no longer have a systematic, age-segregated Sunday school. So you can see where this example is going.) You would think adding another class in the mix would be no big deal. You would also think that a class that was growing would be no big deal either. This class was growing, and God was doing great things in the midst of those attending, but some had problems with it.

You may be wondering, *Well, if you just added a class and it was a growing class, how could it have ever started problems?* The class and the families in the class weren't the ones starting any dissension. It came from others outside the class, particularly those families who kept sending their kids to their age-segregated children's and youth Sunday-school classes as well as adults who were over those same classes.

One comment that surfaced was that the Family Class was hurting the children's and youth ministries of the church. The issue wasn't that the church was losing children numerically. In fact, the Family Class had close to thirty children of all ages present and was actually seeing an increase of families, youth, and children. The problem came from a mind-set that the children belong to the church and not the parents. Some apparently did not think that a child attending Sunday school with his or her parents could be considered to be in children's Sunday school.

The Lord gave me an understanding of what was really going on because we as leaders became increasingly perplexed at the animosity from some who were traveling on the old ship with those who were traveling on this new multigenerational ship. Wouldn't you think people would be happy that finally parents, specifically men, were taking responsibility for the spiritual development of their own children? It was truly asinine. The example of what follows may be a little harsh, but it is exactly what transpired here, and it is why my answer changed from yes to no in answering the million dollar question.

If someone who doesn't drink attends a business social, a party, or even a family function where alcohol is being served, he or she knows from firsthand experience that even when one politely turns down the offer of an alcoholic beverage, friends, coworkers, and/or family members will keep offering a drink. They might say, "C'mon, are you sure you don't want anything? Why don't you just have one?" And they are just as persistent with asking someone if he or she wants a drink as that individual is persistent with telling them no. Several things will happen because the individual consistently refuses the offer to drink. First, so-called friends may decide not to be friends any more. Second, those same friends may have to let others know that Mr. or Mrs. Goodie Two-Shoes refuses to drink. And third, the nondrinker will probably be the last person to know about the next office Christmas party or family reunion.

Why can't the person with a drink in hand simply respect the nondrinker's decision to abstain from drinking alcohol? I believe the answer is found in 1 Peter 3:14–16.

> Even if you should suffer for righteousness' sake, you will be blessed. Have no fear of them, nor be troubled, but in your hearts honor Christ the Lord as holy, always being prepared to make a defense to anyone who asks you for a reason for the hope that is in you; yet do it with gentleness and respect, having a good conscience, so that, when you are slandered, those who revile your good behavior in Christ may be put to shame.

Somehow subconsciously the principle of this Scripture plays out. The nondrinker's refusal to participate in the consumption of alcohol causes the drinker to experience shame and to slander the nondrinker. The drinker's conscience has been seared while the nondrinker's conscience is clean. Seemingly, the only way to clear the drinker's conscience is to have the nondrinker compromise his or her conscience and morals by drinking.

Returning back to our church experience, it was almost like the parents who said no to having their children separated from them during the Sunday-school hour or for any other segregated children's program received similar persecution from those who were still drinking from the sour cistern of the segregated ministries. First, those in the segregated ministries started to distance themselves almost subconsciously from the people in the Family Class. Next, they started to make comments to others about those in the Family Class. Third, they became secretive amongst themselves and found other socials and churches to attend. The same pattern existed in the lives of these church members that I described in my example of the one who was drinking.

When some of the families started to take responsibility and raise their children differently, some of the other families who would not take the biblical responsibility of evangelizing and discipling their own children almost acted as if they were shamed. It was as if their consciences became seared.

I have been told that comparing drinking to sending children to age-segregated activities is a little insensitive. Let me say a couple of things. Number one, by using that example I am in no way saying it is okay to drink or it is okay to go to places where drinking is going on. Number two, I am not making a moral equivalency between someone who drinks alcohol and someone who sends his or her children and youth to be taught by someone else. I am simply stating that the spiritual principle in 1 Peter can be seen in both instances; the person who has chosen a better way to live often receives some sort of persecution from someone who knows that there is a better way but refuses to do what it takes to better themselves and/or their families. It probably would have been a lot easier to use Voddie Baucham's illustration of creating a Junior Varsity Team and a Varsity Team under the same roof of a church. That is exactly what transpired here. The JV team held animosity against the Varsity team, but the JVers weren't willing to do what it takes to be Varsity lettermen.[1]

If you want to put my theory that you will be ostracized for choosing to live a certain better way to the test, then go ahead and live differently. Become radical for Jesus. Educate your children biblically under your tutelage in your home. Keep your kids out of children's church and other segregated children's classes at church. Don't let your teenagers date. Instead, be a family who practices courtship. Don't let your kids go off to summer church camp. Turn the TV off and read nightly together as a family and practice home worship. Be fruitful and multiply and open your home to the blessings of more children. Tell the Awana director politely that your children do not need their program because of the catechism and Scripture memorization they are getting at home.

Go ahead and try it. Then e-mail me and tell me how long it was before you started to face questioning and ridicule from people in your own church. Try it. I double-dog dare you. Reread 1 Peter 3:14–16 and don't be surprised. Rather, be encouraged and empowered. Amen.

Same Words, But Not the Same Meaning

The fundamental reason I believe that a true multigenerational church can't exist under the same roof of the segregated, institutionalized church of our day is that to truly understand both would be to know that they are fundamentally different. Although the language and words used to describe each are often the same, those words have different meanings depending upon what side of the fence you are on. A common frustration that our members of Ridgewood express now is that people just don't get it and that it seems when they talk to others about church, they are talking about two very different things.

I have a very good friend in the ministry, Jay McSwain, and he has kept up with all that God has done and is doing in our midst here at Ridgewood. He is and has been a constant ear, a consistent encourager, and even a challenging debater with me through this journey. Recently, in one of our long phone conversations, Jay made a comment (an *Aha!* moment as he would call it) that showed that he indeed got it. We were talking about an acquaintance of ours who was intrigued about the change at our church. This acquaintance's church was doing a lot of great multigenerational things: one being having a church-wide, multigenerational mission trip. This church would be considered more family friendly than most, and there is no doubt they have started to turn the ship. But in comparing the two churches, Jay made the following comment: "Dustin, what you guys are calling a family church and what these guys are calling a family church are two totally different things."

Ding, ding, ding. My buddy Jay wins the prize. He gets it. One of the reasons I have written this book and have shared quite openly and honestly with you our journey is so that you too will get it. We are not talking about a fad, a program, a process, or even a model. We are simply talking about being a biblical, healthy church. We are talking about belonging to a local body of believers who desire to corporately pursue holiness and righteousness together in order for the gospel to spread to the uttermost parts of the earth in supernatural power. We are talking about seeing His kingdom come here on earth as it is in heaven as we eagerly await the coming of the King of Kings and Lord of Lords for His church: His pure and spotless bride.

Chapter 11

What Does the Age-Integrated Church Look Like?
Masks Have Been Removed and Individualism Has Died

In discussing with others our journey as a church, we often see raised eyebrows. If the raised eyebrows are accompanied with a sigh and the rolling of the eyes, we know that we probably need to start talking about the weather. Raised eyebrows with pursed lips and a slight "hmph" usually mean the individual is intrigued and wants to hear more about the changes we have gone through. He or she usually asks, "What does that look like?" The idea of an age-integrated approach to church makes sense to them and seems right, but they just don't know what it looks like. We tell them that we didn't quite know what it looked like either, but once we began to see it unfolding before our own eyes, it was a wondrous sight to behold.

You may have even been wondering to yourself, *What does a multigenerational community of believers look like? What does a Sunday morning look like when you gather? Is it making a difference in people's lives?* I will give you a glimpse into some of the discoveries we have found here at

Ridgewood Church. I am not going to lay out for you everything that goes on and exactly how we do things. You can refer to the next chapter to understand why I will not give you a running list of the exact details of how things operate here each week for there is no magic formula or groundbreaking model to be mimicked. As a side note, if you are looking for an overview of distinctive characteristics and guiding principles of the family-integrated church, then I refer you to chapter 10 of Dr. Baucham's book *Family Driven Faith*. In the meantime, I will talk about some of the aspects of church life at Ridgewood because *Turning the Ship* is about our specific journey.

The Church Masks Have Come Off

I want to first stress that one of the greatest things that has happened in discovering the new land of age integration is that the proverbial church masks have been removed. When a community of believers actually function as a community, it is very hard for anyone to play games. When all ages and all families interact together, it is hard to put on the church mask that tells everyone on Sunday mornings that you are just swell and that you are the model Christian husband, father, wife, mother, daughter, son, or whatever.

Let me give you a scenario depicting how the modern-day church that is institutionalized and segregated makes it easy for someone to wear a mask. Church Joe has been faithful at his church for several decades. He is there every time the door is open, and he proudly tithes to the penny. Joe has taught Sunday school in the children's department for years. Everyone is always so impressed with Joe's knowledge of the weekly lesson in the Sunday-school quarterly and his down-to-earth approach with communicating that knowledge to the children of the church. While Joe is teaching in the children's department, his wife Jane sits in the same chair in her women's Sunday-school class week in and week out. For years Jane has sat in this same chair with her hands properly laid in her lap and a smile on her face. Jane silently smiles and nods every time someone brags about her husband's teaching ability, his love for the children in his class, and his faithfulness to the church. Jane smiles and nods because that is all she can do. She hears the accolades about her husband, but she cannot express the same adoration for her husband.

Jane knows the real Joe. She knows the Joe who treats her harshly each and every day. She knows that the man who will do anything for anybody at the church demands to be waited on hand and foot under the roof of their house. She knows that the same man who is meek and mild with other people's children is callous and overcritical toward their own children. She knows that their own children despised their dad when they were young, and they have rebelled against him and the church now that they are adults. She knows that the man who is such a great Bible teacher one hour a week at church has never even taught the Bible to his wife or his own children at home. He who is a jolly man at church is a jerk at home. Jane always gets ill when Joe stands up at church and tells people what God has told him for she has never seen him pray a day in his life. Week after week, Jane wears a mask at church in order to allow her husband to wear his. After all, if she said anything about who Joe really is, would anyone believe her? How would the church fill his teaching position in the children's department? Jane doesn't want to mess up the weekly operation of the church, so she quietly grows cold, bitter, and angry—all with a smile. After all, she learned her "everything's dandy" smile from one of the best in the church: her husband, Joe.

This is just one example of Sunday-morning masks. It would be a far-fetched example if only you were not thinking of people like Joe and Jane that you have encountered during your years at church. It is very easy to wear a mask in the modern-day program-driven, institutionalized church.

The masks at Ridgewood quickly came off during this directional change. With the purposeful ridding of programs and age-segregated classes, there were no more "service" opportunities, departments, or positions to hide behind. Unlike with the case of Joe and Jane, husbands, wives, and children are now together in all church functions for everyone to see how they interact with each other. Before, Joe and Jane only had to sit by each other during the big church hour where thankfully they didn't have to interact with each other. All they had to do was smile.

It can be scary when masks are torn off. Real problems come to the surface, anguish and pain can be seen, and blemishes are noticed. Often when we are exposed for who we really are, we feel vulnerable and insecure. Let's be frank; the reason we like to hide behind masks is that without them, we are ugly.

The irony is that having our ugliness revealed has led to having our beauty restored. We have had more genuine opportunities to carry one another's burdens, to pray together, to weep together, to rejoice together, to confess to one another, to support one another, and to challenge one another. Becoming a multigenerational community of believers has enabled us to simply become one big family. We all know from experience that the hardest people to deceive are always the people in our families.

The removal of masks has ushered in the beauty of accountability through small, gender-specific accountability groups that meet outside the walls of the church. The beauty of authentic fellowship has blossomed with a church-wide fellowship luncheon that is held each and every Sunday. The beauty of men discipling their wives and children has ushered in the move of God in the homes of these families, our church family, and our community like nothing we had ever seen in our previous church structure. The beauty of children having hearts for God, His Word, His people, and their own parents and siblings is flying in the face of the cultural norm of rebellious and ungrateful children. The beauty of women rejecting the oppression of being raised in a militant feministic society and embracing the freedoms and empowerment of God's roles for them as mothers and wives is creating untold witnessing opportunities for these women with other ladies in our area. The beauty of truly being pro-life is causing families to enlarge because children are a blessing and heritage from the Lord. The beauty of a biblical worldview in God's people is creating fruitful and productive discussions about life in general and the day we live in. The beauty of laborers having a renewed understanding of missions and evangelism is causing boldness in gospel sharing by the laborers out in the harvest fields. The beauty of guests who attend our gatherings being overwhelmed with the sight and true feel of unity in the presence of young and old alike worshipping together is giving power to the testimony of the resurrected Lord. The beauty of households opening up in the spirit of biblical hospitality is creating increased openings for the gospel to be shared with family members, neighbors, and coworkers. The list could go on and on.

God makes all things new and beautiful, and He has done and is doing just that in this multigenerational community of believers. My prayer is that every local body of believers would experience becoming more beautiful through the removal of masks that are so easy to hide behind in the modern-day program-driven age-segregated church.

The Spirit of Individualism Has Died

The spirit of individualism is alive and well in our society, and if we are honest, it is alive and well in the church culture as well. Individualism defined is the belief in the primary importance of the individual and in the virtues of self-reliance and personal independence. There is one difference between individualism in the culture outside the church and the one inside the church. It is the word *God*.

The world says, "I have a plan and purpose for my life." The church says, "I know God has a plan and purpose for my life." You may say, "Amen. What's the problem with the church statement?" The problem is not necessarily in the difference of the two statements, but in their similarities. The personal pronouns of *I* and *my* are the same; hence, the goal of individual pursuit and importance is the same. One just attributes the self-centered plan to a higher power.

Now before your blood starts boiling, let us return back to Church Joe and Church Jane and look at a scenario of how the spirit of individualism can actually short-circuit the fullness of the Lord's plan and purpose for His children. (Please note that I just said that God has a plan and purpose for His children . . . it simply needs to be defined by the totality of His Word and redemptive purposes and not by the humanistic philosophies of our day.)

Here's the example: Joe and Jane are married and attend church faithfully. Joe and Jane are excited about the new campaign at church that will help them discover God's plan and purpose for their lives. Joe and Jane arrive and receive their own books/workbooks which will enable them to seek after God's plan for their individual lives. Joe discovers his, I mean "God's," plan for Joe. Jane discovers the plan for Jane.

Joe and Jane, when talking to each other, discover that their individual plans lead them down paths that will be apart from each other. The two who are supposed to be one are now driving in opposite directions all in the name of God's purpose for their respective individual lives. And by the way, I forgot to mention that Joe and Jane have children. (They were off watching a kid's video in a secluded location in the building while Joe and Jane were learning about God's plan for their lives.)

Jane realizes immediately that she would be free to live out her purpose if she wasn't so tied up with her kids. Joe realizes the pastor's, I mean "God's," plan will require him to be at the church several nights a week and it would be a lot easier if his wife Jane didn't expect him to spend so much time with her and the kids. Shall I go on?

Based on these examples, you can begin to see the error of individualism in the modern church. You may say, "Dustin, you are flirting with being an extremist again!" Well then, I'll be pragmatic in telling you that I can name a handful of families in my nine years of ministry/counseling that have divorced because "God" was leading them to follow "Him" down different paths of service all in "His" name and for "His" church.

In becoming an age-integrated church, we have been forced to confront the affront of individualism in the church at large. We have been on the front lines of battling individualism by rediscovering the beauty of biblical manhood and womanhood. The newfound discovery and understanding of what a biblical man and a biblical woman should be has had a direct effect on the context of our most intimate relationships we as believers have: the relationship with the family.

It was only after we started as a church to equip and train households to relate and function together according to God's design that we were able to properly relate to and with other families and households that comprised the church we belonged to. When individualism died, relationships with others started thriving. Believers were now discovering that God's plans and purposes for their lives were not hindered by those close to them; rather, His plans and purposes included those people whom God had placed in their lives.

A Priceless Testimony of What It Now Looks Like

Although I may not have answered the question of this chapter with specific details about our weekly and yearly schedule, I hope you have gotten just a small glimpse of the land we have discovered. It is no doubt different and is both beautiful and enlightening. Phoniness (masks) and selfishness (individualism) have no place in a body of believers who are nothing more than a family of families. Since there are no systematic, age-segregated departments and ministries, there is no competition for volunteers and money. Instead of working against each other and in spite of others, we are now working with each other and serving each other as well. It has been truly an amazing and liberating journey.

To give you one last glimpse into our new life as an age-integrated church, I want to close with a testimony from someone else that came at a time when great encouragement was needed to stay the course. While I and about nine others were out of the country on a mission trip to Costa Rica, I got word by e-mail that a couple of longtime members had decided to jump ship. Another one of our pastors and his wife were on the mission trip, and I shared with them in the evening the e-mail I had received. This news hit them hard because one of the families was close to them, and it had now been revealed that this leaving family had spoken lies. We were no doubt tired from a long day of evangelizing and gospel distributing in this foreign land, and the enemy was trying to burst our bubble by his workings back home. It was at this moment that the Lord used the testimony of the pastor's wife to prove that He was indeed moving and that we must continue to move with Him.

With tears in her eyes, she proceeded to share with her husband and me a testimony that she shared with the missionary that was leading our team earlier that day. You see, this pastor at Ridgewood and his wife were once international missionaries, and they knew firsthand both the challenges and joys of leaving the United States to live in a foreign land for the sake of the gospel.

Her testimony went something like this, "I was just telling the missionary earlier today about how awesome it is to be a part of our church family back home. I told him that we belong to a church in the US that actually mirrors what it is like to live overseas full time doing missions. Our church families would have no problem adjusting to the demands of picking up all they have and doing missions in a foreign land."

What this pastor's wife was talking about is the reality that it is hard for a family to leave their church in the United States to go onto the mission field full time. It is hard because the U.S. family would not have the same church structure and system to be a part of on foreign soil. The wife and mother would not have her little class with women all who have children of the same age, and the children, especially the teens, would not have their youth group to be there for them in this new land. This U.S. family that has accepted the call to missions would have to attend a church gathering possibly in a home with other believers, and possibly for the first time in their lives would now have to attend church together as a family. The family would have to be their own support group; this too would be a first.

In contrast, Christians from age-integrated or family-integrated churches already function as their own support group by learning, worshipping, and growing together and regularly interacting with other families and people of all ages.

Her testimony on that evening came at the right time and was worth more than money, success, or notoriety could buy. That testimony is the best answer I can give you or anyone when the question is asked, "What does it look like?"

Chapter 12

You Can't Buy It in a Box
Where to Go from Here

Through the process of seeing the ship turned in our church, we have had many fellow believers and church leaders seek us out inquiring about what God is doing through these changes. The hearts of these believers are overwhelmed with the current state of Christianity, and their eyes have been opened toward the fact that a drastic change needs to take place. They offer up a common question that shows, however, that their minds are lagging behind both their hearts and eyes. The mind-numbing question is, "How do we add this multigenerational approach in our church?" Let me decipher this question for you: "Is there a program or campaign that we can do at our church that will help us change to this direction?" This question shows just how much we have checked in our brains in our church life.

In checking in our brains, we have essentially forfeited the direct access that we as believers have with the One who imparts heavenly wisdom. We are frivolously looking for the latest and greatest ministry plan that can help our churches grow. In this pursuit, we often turn to the ideas of mere men instead of the impeccable guidance from our majestic Maker.

We are quick to turn to a specific ministry in a box instead of relying upon what is already contained in the great Book.

Before you start saying that I am too hard on all these well-meaning, inquisitive believers, let me just say that I am speaking from experience. In the early stages of our directional change, our hearts were desperate and our eyes were eager to see things happen. Our minds, being plagued with years in modern church approaches and programs, were frustrated and flustered. We wanted a script to follow that we could buy at the local Christian bookstore or find online. We didn't know what to do or where to start. We had been so accustomed to having access to canned church programs for all ages and occasions that we were disappointed that we could find no such thing to help us now with this new direction. To put it plainly, we were blithering idiots without a clue. We wanted everything to be laid out step-by-step for us.

God Imparts Wisdom to His Children

Of course as you've gathered, there was no top-ten-things-to-do list for us as we traveled in the new direction of becoming an age-integrated community of believers. We didn't know any of the hot-button words such as *multigenerational* or *family integrated*. We turned to the Lord in prayer and we sought for direction and confirmation from His Word. We did exactly what James 1:5–6 admonishes. "If any of you lacks wisdom, let him ask God, who gives generously to all without reproach, and it will be given him. But let him ask in faith, with no doubting, for the one who doubts is like a wave of the sea that is driven and tossed by the wind."

Repentance and Humility Were His Answer

We prayed, and God imparted His wisdom. He required us as leaders to be broken. People want to know how we have communicated with the congregation during this change. I always answer them that we communicated honestly with them. We had to tell people that we too, as leaders, had to learn to lead our families. We had to confess that in all of our years in ministry, we had never been equipped to evangelize and disciple our own children. We had never learned how to lead our families in home worship. We had to communicate to them with utter humility that we were learning with them as we moved forward.

We didn't act like we knew all the answers, and we didn't even act like we knew what things would look like one year or two years down the road. We had to ask for forgiveness for being a part of the problem with the statistical loss of our young people over the previous decade.

I remember asking one family for forgiveness because of how we as staff in the past had talked about them being paranoid parents. You see, these parents were the parents who never let their teens sit with the youth in church and never let their children go on any youth event overnight. Some still may say they were just overprotective, but I will tell you today that they were right in their parental decision making. I commended them on their parenting now instead of criticizing them. I have no doubt that their children will defy the grim odds of leaving the faith as they enter their adult lives.

Alleluia! We Are Not Alone!

Although we now know that what has transpired here at Ridgewood has been termed the family-integrated church movement, I am thankful to this day that this journey started without any particular model or plan for us to follow. I say this not to boast in what has happened, but to tell you that it is a pretty awesome feeling to know that despite what any critic may say, what has happened here can only be attributed to the sovereign move of God. We were doing things before we even knew we were supposed to do them.

I will also be the first to tell you that we were more than delighted to find out that we were not alone in this journey. Pastor Kyle was at a conference for our state convention, and he was talking to a convention worker about the direction we felt the Lord was leading us as well as our struggle of feeling all alone in this journey. This worker and good friend encouraged Kyle that we should stay the course. He said that what Kyle was describing to him seemed to be happening elsewhere. He referred Kyle and our church to Josh McDowell's *Last Christian Generation* which at the time was hot off the press. This book was a great encouragement to us.

Then not too long after this encounter, a message preached by Dr. Voddie Baucham at our state's evangelism conference was sparking debates across our denomination. When we got a copy of this message entitled "The Centrality of the Home," we knew for sure that we were a part of something big. We were no longer the only ones out in left field, and we were finding that the company out there was pretty good. (To view this message by Dr. Baucham, visit http://www.gracefamilybaptist.net/GFBC_/Podcast/Entries/2008/1/11_The_Centrality_of_the_Home.html.)

Since then, we have been introduced to the National Council of Family-Integrated Churches and a whole host of believers who are making this same journey. The knowledge that God is indeed moving strengthens us daily.

To-Do List or Not-to-Do List

When I started to write this book, I started to write a to-do list at the end of the first chapter with the plan of having a to-do list at the end of every chapter. To be honest with you, a to-do list would be easy for me to come up with and put on paper for you. But if I did that, I would be stealing from you the joy of thinking. I would be guilty of putting Dustin's thoughts in a "box." I, the author, would be telling you exactly what you should be getting out of your reading. I would be thinking for you. This is a common occurrence in modern-day books. At the end of each chapter of a lot of church books, there is either a to-do list or study questions.

I am not opposed to this practice and have even benefited from many of the lists in books I've read. I do, however, feel that these lists contribute to the mental apathy that prevails in Christendom. We no longer know how to dissect information for ourselves. We are always looking for the quick fix and the easy way out. These lists often do the nitty-gritty work for us. We long for the magic ministry "box" that will put our churches, as well as us, on the map. (If you think I am stretching this idea of ministry in a "box," it may help you to know that there is an actual product on the market entitled "Youth Ministry in a Box." I'm not joking.)

Where Do I Go From Here?

God is looking for a people who will turn to Him and seek His face. He is looking for a people who will ask Him for wisdom. He is looking for a people who will be transformed by the renewing of their minds and actually have their mental capacities awakened.

There is a song I want to leave you with in response to the question, "Where do I go from here?" It is a song written and recorded by Ross King. My prayer and challenge to you is that these words would be your prayer as you seek the Lord's will in your life, your family's life, and the life of your church. The words of this song say in just a few words what I have been trying to get across with the many words of this book.

Truth Unending
Ross King

Show me all the lies that I'm believing
I desire to live in truth
No matter what the cost
Shine your light upon
The darkest places hidden in my heart

(Chorus)
Consume my thoughts
Because I know You desire to set me free
With truth unending
And it gives me hope
Because I know You can do
More than I believe
So I'm depending
On You alone

Show me all the idols I've bowed down to
I desire to live in truth
No matter what the cost
Shine your light upon
The darkest places hidden in my heart

(Chorus)[1]

Chapter 13

God Help Me. Amen.
Closing Remarks

I may be young, but I am not dumb. I know full well that this book will not be well received by many. I know it will probably be mocked as elementary and naïve by those who are neck deep in the workings of our modern-day institutionalized churches and denominations. If I ever thought I had a chance to speak at the big conferences, that chance has most likely been washed down the drain with this book as well. So be it.

I can honestly say that I and my family will never go back to a church life with segregated ministries and programs that is the norm in our current church culture. I don't say this with pride; rather, I make this statement and claim with humility and deep conviction. I don't say this with ignorance; rather, I say this with the same understanding and resolve that I had some fourteen years ago when I broke away from the Roman Catholic Church, the faith of my childhood and family for generations.

To all who have ears to hear, I close with the same words spoken by Martin Luther at the Diet of Worms as he traveled against the current of the church culture of his day some five hundred years ago:

> *Unless I am convinced by Scripture and plain reason—I do not accept the authority of the popes and councils, for they have contradicted each other—my conscience is captive to the Word of God. I cannot and I will not recant anything for to go against conscience is neither right nor safe. God help me. Amen.*
>
> *Martin Luther, April 16, 1521*

Notes

Foreword

1. George Whitefield, "The Great Duty of Family Religion."
2. Richard Baxter, *The Reformed Pastor* (Edinburgh, Scotland: Banner of Truth, 1979).
   The term "family religion" is a common reference to the daily practice of family worship (prayer, Bible reading, singing, and catechism) that was common practice among Christian families prior to the modern era.
3. I use the term neo-traditional to denote the fact that the age-integrated model is in fact the traditional, New Testament model, and the age-segregated model has merely assumed the mantle of "traditional" church in very recent church history.

Chapter 1

1. Barna, George. *Think Like Jesus: Make the Right Decision Every Time* (Brentwood: Integrity, 2003), 22.
2. Rainer, Thomas S. *The Bridger Generation* (Nashville: Broadway & Holman, 2006), 169.

3. Shultz, Glenn. *Kingdom Education* (Nashville: Lifeway, 2005), 98. See also the 2002 Report of the Southern Baptist Council on Family Life.
4. McDowell, Josh. *The Last Christian Generation* (Holiday: Green Key, 2006), 15.
5. Ibid, 17.
6. Ibid, 15.
7. Henry, Matthew. *Matthew Henry's Commentary: Volume 6—Acts to Revelation* (Peabody: Hendrickson, 1991), 368.

Chapter 2

1. Hybels, Bill. "The Wake-up Call of My Adult Life." Spoken at 2007 Leadership Summit. This can be viewed at http://revealnow.com/story.asp?storyid=49.
2. Ibid.
3. Ibid.
4. Visit www.pragmatism.org and http://dewey.pragmatism.org for more study.
5. *The Oxford Pocket Dictionary of Current English* (Oxford University Press, 2008).
6. Wagner, C. Peter. *Your Church Can Grow—Seven Vital Signs of a Healthy Church* (Eugene: Wipf and Stock, 1981), 161.
7. Hoyle, Jeff. "Focus on the Family, Church Outreach," Focus on the Family Webinar, Slide 21, 2007.
8. Schaeffer, Franky. *Addicted to Mediocrity: 20th Century Christians and the Arts* (Wheaton: Good News, 1981), 45.
9. Lael Weinberger's article "Evolution in American education and the demise of its public school system." http://www.answersingenesis.org/docs2005/0131education.asp

10. Pamphlet, "If Evolution is right, how can everyone be so wrong?" http://www.jeremiah7.com/jeremiah_7_tracts/download_evolution_handout.pdf
11. Loeffler, John. "Worldview Wars: Paradigms, Preaching, and Politics," www.khouse/org/articles/2001/365/
12. Brisbane, Holly E. *The Developing Child* (Peoria: Chas. A. Bennet, 1965), 17–18.
13. *The Gingerbread Man.* Pictures by Karen Lee Schmidt (New York: Scholastic). Text copyright 1967. Illustrations copyright 1985.

Chapter 3

1. Calvin, John. *Calvin's Commentaries: Acts 14–28 & Romans 1–16*, ed. John Owen (Grand Rapids: Baker Book House, 1996), 454.
2. *Examining Youth Ministry Forum: Discovering a Biblical Paradigm for Youth Ministry.* December 7, 2006. Voddie Baucham presentation. 4-DVD set can be purchased at http://www.planetstudents.org/PS_resources.php.
3. *Webster's Dictionary: New Encyclopedic Edition* (Canada: McGraw-Hill, 2001), 302.
4. McArthur, John. *How to Get the Most Out of God's Word* (Dallas: Word, 1997), 35.
5. Henry, Matthew. *Matthew Henry's Commentary: Volume 1—Genesis to Deuteronomy* (Peabody: Hendrickson, 1991), 668.
6. Ibid.

Chapter 5

1. "2002 Annual Church Profile Statistics: Number of Baptisms by Age." http://www.namb.net/atf/cf/%7BCDA250E8-8866-4236-9A0C-C646DE153446%7D/2002_AgeGroup_BAPTISMS.pdf
2. Schaff, Philip. *History of the Christian Church: Volume I, Apostolic Christianity* (Grand Rapids: Wm. B. Eerdmans, 1910, 1995), 248.
3. Schaeffer, Francis. *How Shall We Then Live? The Rise and Decline of Western Thought and Culture* (Wheaton: Crossway, 1976), 227.
4. MacArthur, John F. *Twelve Ordinary Men* (Nashville: W Publishing, 2002), 11.

Chapter 6

1. Mayhue, Richard L. "Rediscovering Expository Preaching." An essay in John MacArthur's *Preaching: How to Preach Biblically* (Nashville: Thomas Nelson, 2005), 10.
2. Ibid, 10.
3. Dever, Mark. *Nine Marks of a Healthy Church* (Wheaton: Crossway, 2004), 40.
4. Ibid, 42.
5. Gill, John. *Exposition of the Old and New Testaments: John to Galatians* (London: Northumberland-Court, 1809), 160.
6. MacArthur, John. *The MacArthur NT Commentary: Acts 1–12* (Chicago: Moody, 1994), 73.
7. Barna, George and Frank Viola. *Pagan Christianity: Exploring the Roots of Our Church Practices* (Wheaton: Tyndale, 2008), 189.

Chapter 7

1. Barna, George. *Revolution* (Wheaton: Tyndale, 2005), 33.

Chapter 8

1. Mayhue, Richard. "Cultivating a Biblical Mind-set." An essay in John MacArthur's *Think Biblically! Rediscovering a Christian Worldview.* John MacArthur, general editor. (Wheaton: Crossway, 2003), 48.

Chapter 9

1. Barna, George. "New Marriage and Divorce Statistics," Released March 31, 2008. http://www.barna.org/FlexPage.aspx?Page=BarnaUpdate&BarnaUpdateID=295
2. Ibid.

Chapter 10

1. Team illustration from conversation between Dr. Voddie Baucham and author.

Chapter 12

1. Words and music by Ross King. Copyright 2000 Ross King (Administered by Ross King). All rights reserved. Used by permission. Visit www.rossking.com to be blessed by his music.

Printed in the United States
141910LV00002B/2/P